Monetary Decisions of the Supreme Court

The Rutgers Banking Series consists of books in the field of American banking which have grown out of research at the Stonier Graduate School of Banking

Monetary Decisions
of the Supreme Court

by

Gerald T. Dunne

Rutgers University Press · *New Brunswick, New Jersey*

Preface

This work traces a series of decisions of the Supreme Court which have raised the monetary power of the United States government from relative insignificance to almost unlimited authority.

The emergence of federal monetary authority provides a vivid illustration of the process of constitutional development. The Constitution says little on the subject, with the result that the Supreme Court has had to say a good deal. The generality of the Constitution on this point is no accident; the Founding Fathers regarded political control of monetary institutions with an abhorrence born of bitter experience, and they seriously considered writing a sharp limitation on such governmental activity into the Constitution itself. Yet they did not, and by "speaking in silences" gave the government they founded the near-absolute authority over currency and coinage that has always been considered the necessary consequence of national sovereignty.

From this obscure origin, the money power developed both as cause and effect of the profound changes in the institution of money that occurred in the ensuing century and a half. The context of this judicial development divides, both chronologically and organically, into two sequences. The first set of decisions grew out of friction of this national power with the residual authority of the states. The second took up where the substance of the first left off and attempted to square the competing demands of public control over the institution of money and individual freedom in its use. The case-by-case nature of this development has made it disjointed and episodic. Yet both sets of adjudications possessed an over-all coherence and direction, and bear out Chief Justice John Marshall's description of the Constitution as an instrument "intended to endure for ages to come, and, consequently, to be adapted to various crises of human affairs."

This book is addressed primarily to the general reader. It is hoped, however, that economists and attorneys will find it of interest since the subject matter, curiously enough, seems to have escaped any extended development by economic historians or writers on constitutional law.

Delineation of these Supreme Court decisions is a formidable task. Each case is saturated in political history. Each involves a tangle of economic factors. Each presents a problem in legal calculus. Consequently, a definitive treatment—which this effort is not—requires an almost encyclopedic detail. There are other handicaps. Judicial writing simply cannot have the clarity and precision of multiplication tables; summarization of its subtlety and complexity (and, alas, its occasional turgidity) is a dangerous business involving distortion at the best and downright error at the worst. Finally, the summarizer inevitably becomes a commentator because he, in the very necessities of the case, has his opinions about the opinions. These judgments seep through all conscious attempts at objectivity and color the drift and direction of his narrative.

Where such judgments appear here, they are personal to the author and do not purport to represent any view of his employer, the Federal Reserve Bank of St. Louis, or of the Stonier Graduate School of Banking, which accepted the original of this work as a thesis. The author's obligation to colleagues, past and present, in the Federal Reserve System

is immense. Special thanks are also due Mrs. Stephen Taraso-
vich, who typed the manuscript and assisted in preparing it
for publication.

GERALD T. DUNNE

May, 1959
St. Louis, Missouri

Contents

Contents

Monetary Decisions of the Supreme Court

1

The money power: background and origin

In the year 1598, the Irish rose in one of their chronic rebellions against the British crown and provoked a reaction that brought not only military repression but economic warfare as well. In order to stretch the royal budget for the Irish war, Queen Elizabeth struck a special coinage which contained less silver and more alloy than that prescribed in the standard English sterling. Use of this "mixed" money was sternly forbidden in England. In Ireland, however, it was proclaimed lawful money and ordered to be "used, accepted, and reputed" as such. In short, it was an occupation currency.

Sometime before this proclamation, an Irish merchant had bought some goods for which he specifically promised to pay one hundred pounds in English sterling. He appeared in Dublin on the day fixed for payment and tendered one hundred pounds—in occupation coinage—in settlement of the debt. The creditor refused to take the debased money and sued for payment in sterling. However, in 1604 the court held for the debtor, and announced as the rule of its decision in the landmark Case of the Mixed Moneys:

. . . as the king by his prerogative may make money of what matter and form he pleases and establish the standard of it, so he may change his money in substance and impression, and enhance or debase the value of it or entirely decry and annul it. . . .

. . . although . . . at the time of contract . . . pure money was current in this kingdom . . . yet mixed money being established . . . before the day of payment . . . may be tendered . . . and the obligee is bound to accept it. . . .[1]

This old case affords a host of insights. One, which should not be labored, is the sheer injustice that can result from changing monetary rules ex post facto. The second is the institution of "legal tender," which is the heart of monetary authority and, consequently, deserves some extended analysis. In its strictest sense "legal tender" is a term of the courtroom; a plea of legal tender is what lawyers call a plea in avoidance. That is to say, it is an admission whose damaging effect is immediately nullified by bringing in some additional facts. Thus, a defendant charged with murder might admit the killing and plead self-defense. Similarly, a defendant charged with debt might admit the borrowing and plead "legal tender"—namely, that at some previous time he physically had offered his creditor money which the law deemed acceptable for debt payments and had been refused. Such a plea, if proved in an early English tribunal, ended the creditor's suit then and there. The court would not aid in the recovery of even debased money once it had been turned down. The creditor's total loss was "accounted his own folly that he had refused the money when a lawful tender of it was made him." [2]

[1] 80 Eng. Rept. 507 (reported in "law" French); Sir John Davies Irish Reports 48 (English translation), 72–77.
[2] Sir Edward Coke, *Institutes* (Philadelphia: Robert H. Small, 1853), II, Sec. 335, p. 207a. This harsh doctrine was later softened to permit a suit after refusal, with the creditor losing post-tender interest and paying all court costs.

But to dwell on the technical aspects of legal tender badly misplaces the emphasis. The legal plea is available because the sovereign authority makes it so. That sovereignty—the crown (or Parliament) in England and, as we shall see, the Congress in the United States—takes such action because there is a doubt that the sovereignty's money is acceptable at face value. Hence, compulsion is brought to bear. In other words, the enactment of legal tender divests rights, otherwise legal and enforcible, that the sovereignty deems repugnant to the public interest. Such rights, of course, can be whittled down or nullified in other ways, as by out-and-out proscription or by withholding remedial legal machinery. The method of nullification is relatively unimportant. The fact of nullification is. And there are two interests under constant pressure to achieve the fact. One is the sovereignty itself, which is not only participant but also referee in the game of getting and spending. The other is the whole debtor class, a term that is by no means synonymous with the poor.

The most important aspect of the Case of the Mixed Moneys, however, is its historical perspective. It shows, for example, both the centralized political despotism and the fledgling free-enterprise economic system that characterized Tudor England. We may note that these institutions flowered from a common root; for when the crown successively crushed baronage and church, it destroyed a society of status and reciprocal obligations. This destruction caused previously diffused political relationships to coalesce in the monarchy, while at the same time inherited economic relationships of status began to dissolve into the negotiated relationships of contract.

The case thus points up the inherent contradiction of these two components of the new order when the centralized political power was exerted along economic lines. The purpose of the debased money—good enough for Ireland, but sternly forbidden in England—was closely associated with a policy under which monopolies were granted, home manufactures encouraged, and a navy and merchant marine established, all to the common end of enhancing the national—as distinguished from regional or individual—interest. And, as we know, within this framework of a closed economic system, gold and silver held almost mystical qualities, being regarded as both the symbol and substance of national prosperity. All effort was bent to its accumulation within the realm, and its export was vigorously discouraged.

Hence, three years before Jamestown, the case forecasts the economic and monetary trend of British colonial enterprise. Colonies were to be satellites, founded as sources of materials and as markets for manufactures. Men and material would go overseas, but not gold and silver. Indeed, the very purpose of the colonial foundation was to make sure that gold and silver came to, rather than left, England.

PRE-CONSTITUTIONAL DEVELOPMENT

Accordingly, the American colonists were caught from the start in monetary difficulties. They had not come to the new continent to re-establish the status society of medieval England, but rather to go forward where England had left off. However, their transplanted economic attitudes presumed a system of metal currency which their world of reality did not, indeed could not, contain. Mining of gold and silver in America was negligible; the precious metals that came from England had to be sent in the teeth of prohibitions by successive English governments. The coin that came from illicit trading with the Spanish colonies in the Caribbean was constantly drained away to England in exchange for English products.

Without a metal medium of exchange, substitutes arose in the colonies. Wampum, tobacco, salt, and other commodities —in short, prehistoric monetary devices—were pressed into service as monetary media.[3] Then, at the close of the seventeenth century, the colonial monetary experiments went to the ultramodern. In 1690 Massachusetts passed a law providing for ten-shilling "indented bills" to pay off the militia. Each bill recited that such sum was due the possessor from the colony and that it would be accepted for that amount for taxes. The bills were thus a legal tender against the issuing colony. Their small face value, the absence of interest, and the tax provision made the bills considerably different from conventional debt instruments. The bills obviously were not to be held for payment but to pass from hand to hand as money.

These original "bills of credit" were, in non-Oriental history at least, apparently the first governmental paper currency issued without metallic backing. The bills set the pattern that would characterize every American monetary development for the next two centuries; for the capabilities of the new instruments were immediately and optimistically comprehended. Although in theory they marked a tremendous monetary advance, their limitations would take generations to overcome. Consequently, trial-and-error development was mostly error, as, for example, when depreciation and additional issues of the Massachusetts paper followed each other in a dreary sequence that was scarcely affected by the colony's action in 1692 to make the bills a "legal tender" for private debt.

At least eight colonies followed Massachusetts' lead and printed paper money; it varied considerably even within a single colony as to quantity, security, redemption, and legal

[3] In Virginia the Established Church was supported by a tax payable in tobacco by communicants and dissenters alike. The rises and falls of the tobacco market compounded the inequitable impact of the levy and, in turn, engendered a growing hostility not only to the tax but to the very institution of a state-supported religion. It was this climate that produced Madison's famous *Memorial Against Religious Assessments* and Jefferson's *Statute of Religious Liberty*, the precursors of the "no establishment" clause of the First Amendment.

tender. The history of these currencies appears as mixed as their characteristics. Some authorities seem to have written off all colonial currencies as an inflationary adventure of the crudest type. Yet other commentators, both contemporary and modern, have attested that certain of the issues were handled not only with competence but with wisdom.[4]

On the other hand, it was undeniable that many issues left much to be desired, and the painful manifestations of a depreciating currency—rising prices, barter transactions, suspicion in business dealings, and general economic derangement—were widespread and recurrent. Writing on the other side of the Atlantic, Adam Smith put his finger on the cause of all the trouble: "A positive law may render a shilling legal tender for a guinea; because it may direct the courts of justice to discharge the debtor who made the tender. But no positive law can oblige a person who sells goods and who is at liberty to sell or not to sell, as he pleases, to accept a shilling as equivalent to a guinea in the price of them."[5]

In the British view, debasement of Irish money was one thing, and debasement of colonial money quite another. The distinction was quite logical and depended on who did the debasing and for what purpose. Since the colonies were regarded as cows to be milked rather than steers to be slaughtered, derangement of orderly economic processes by way of unauthorized monetary meddling was intolerable. If any-

---

[4] Maryland seems to have come off particularly well (see Clarence P. Gould, *Money and Transportation in Maryland* [Baltimore: The Johns Hopkins Press, 1915]); and Pennsylvania was astonishingly successful in achieving economic expansion within a framework of general price stability (see Richard A. Lester, "Currency Issues to Overcome Depressions in Pennsylvania, 1723 and 1729," *Journal of Political Economy*, XLVI [June, 1938], 324–375). Perhaps the most striking tribute to the Pennsylvania experiment is Adam Smith's grudging and implicit endorsement contained in his three references to it in *The Wealth of Nations* (Modern Library edition, New York: Random House, 1937, pp. 310–311, 772, and 893). It is difficult to determine the extent to which the Pennsylvania issues were legal tender, but the very difficulty seems to show that legal tender is a matter of real controversy only when a money loses value.
[5] *The Wealth of Nations*, p. 311.

thing, the British reaction seems surprisingly mild. It came in successive statutes, which first banned additional issues of paper money in New England and then prohibited all further colonial legal tender laws.[6] The supposed economic remedy only served to irritate deteriorating political relationships. Although the British never yielded on legal tender, they made some subsequent monetary concessions. Like the rest of their abortive policy of conciliation, the gesture was too slight and too late.

Political and economic differences flared into war, and "the rattle of the musketry near Boston was quickly followed by the rattle of the printing presses from New Hampshire to South Carolina"[7] when the colonies and their Continental Congress turned to bills of credit as the principal means of financing the war. Congressional action was somewhat premature, for the central government was not given such specific power until 1777 under the ninth Article of Confederation. It used the authority up to the hilt, denouncing anyone who refused to take its continental dollar "as an enemy of the liberties of the United States," and requesting the states—sometimes with success—to make its paper a legal tender.

The economic dislocation of the six-year revolution was intensified by these swollen issues of paper money, and they had virtually exhausted themselves by the time peace and independence came. The continental dollar was paid off at one-fortieth of par, in the face of the twelfth Article of Confederation asserting "the solemn pledge" of "the United States and the public faith" for payment and satisfaction. The colonies, now sovereign states, were, monetarily, in about

[6] 4 Geo. II 53 (1751) and 4 Geo. III 34 (1764). Adam Smith reflected sentiment on both sides when he noted: "No law could be more equitable than the act of Parliament, so unjustly complained of in the colonies, which declared no paper currency to be emitted there in the time coming, should be a legal tender of payment." *The Wealth of Nations*, p. 311.
[7] Allan Nevins, *The American States During and After the Revolution, 1775–1789* (New York: The Macmillan Company, 1924), p. 420.

the same low position. They were slightly, and only slightly, better off, since they had supplemented their paper financing with some taxation (which the Continental Congress could not do) and afterwards attained a precarious financial stability by using confiscated Tory property to redeem their currency to a limited extent. Yorktown and the peace treaty ended the fighting, but chaotic monetary conditions continued through the first years of independence.

We can sum up the pre-constitutional monetary history of the United States as an experience which contained far more failures than successes and which wound up with hyperinflation. Trade was at a near standstill. Economic rivalries cut across state lines as the country was beset by controversies over existing currency and tender laws. There were successive waves of agitation, and indeed even armed insurrection, for additional ones. The benefits of national independence were being frittered away by bickering among the states (including attempts to stamp out each other's money) and an impotent central government. Fulfillment of the great promise of an untapped continent was delayed, it seemed, by the absence of a workable financial mechanism. Monetary woes were only part of the troubles of the young country but were an accurate index of disunion and inertia.

THE CONSTITUTIONAL CONVENTION

The Congress shall have Power . . . To Coin Money, regulate the Value thereof, and of foreign Coin. . . .—United States Constitution, Article I, Section 8, Clause 5.

No State shall . . . coin Money; emit Bills of Credit; make any Thing but gold and silver Coin a Tender in Payment of Debts; pass any Bill of Attainder, ex post facto Law, or Law impairing the Obligation of Contracts. . . . —United States Constitution, Article I, Section 10, Clause 1.

In the late spring of 1787, fifty-five men from twelve states met in Philadelphia to try to do something about the host of problems besetting the country. The money problem was with them from the first, being reflected even on the roster of delegates. Rhode Island, the stronghold of a paper money party, scented monetary reform in the air and refused to participate. The tiny state's suspicion was certainly justified when keynoter Edmund Randolph inveighed against "the havoc of paper money" in his indictment of the Articles of Confederation.[8] The audience needed no reminder. Every man present could personally testify to the convulsive monetary situation. Some could speak of its compounded injustice, as, for example, Washington, who had refused compensation for his Revolutionary service, then come home to have his mortgages paid off in Virginia paper worth ten cents on the dollar.

Madison later summed up the general sentiment in his excoriation of pre-constitutional paper money as a pestilence which inflicted nothing but destruction "on the necessary confidence between man and man, on the necessary confidence in the public councils, on the industry and morals of the people, and on the character of republican government."[9] Yet the audience also included theorists, who were able to distinguish between the excesses of a paper currency and the obvious role that this medium would have to play in any future national monetary mechanism.[10] Certainly, Franklin and Hamilton, who possessed intellectual and practical genius of the highest order, grasped the three-dimensional monetary

---

[8] *Documents Illustrative of the Formation of the Union of the American States* (House Document No. 398, 69th Congress, 1st Session, 1927), p. 115.

[9] *The Federalist*, No. 44.

[10] A somewhat misleading but technically correct statement would be that half of the American monetary theorists of any note were present. Professor Mints singles out eight men as contributors to early American monetary thought (*A History of Banking Theory* [Chicago: University of Chicago Press, 1945], pp. 62–63); four of them—Franklin, Hamilton, Gouverneur Morris, and Thomas Fitzsimmons—were delegates to the Convention.

problem: the linkage of money and government finance; the indispensability of money to economic expansion; and the destruction potential of money as an instrument of expropriation.

Given recognition of the problem and men with versatile genius to work out a solution, the Constitutional Convention could be expected to come up with explicit answers to the money question in fairly short order. Actually, the opposite turned out to be the case. Discussions were sporadic and often inconclusive. The experts were silent. The clauses concerning monetary affairs seem to have been put into the Constitution in an almost offhand manner.

It was midsummer before the Convention came to grips with this issue. On August 16 the drafting committee brought in its proposals on congressional powers. One of these was practically a reproduction of the old Article of Confederation authorizing Congress to coin money and emit bills of credit. As we read Madison's notes of the proceedings, we are struck by the fact that the paper money proposal touched off simultaneous debates on two related but distinct proposals. One was to strike the authority from the draft. The other was to go even further and write a positive prohibition on paper money into the Constitution. Gouverneur Morris backed the proposed deletion on the ground that the authority would be useless, asserting that if the government had credit, bills of credit were unnecessary, and if it did not, the bills were a mockery. Another delegate agreed, pointing out that the power to issue bills was already included in the power of borrowing.

Other observations were more vehement than enlightening. One man compared bills of credit to the mark of the beast of Revelations. A second proposed rejecting the whole Constitution if it retained the paper money authority. A third begged the assembly to shut and bar the door against paper money. James Madison attempted to compose differences by suggesting that the prohibition be confined to legal tender. One self-styled friend of paper money—who seemed to be a very lonely man—pointed out that any such action would alienate debtors in the forthcoming struggle to adopt the Constitution. Another delegate, likewise concerned with ratification, observed that leaving in the bills of credit clause would outrage creditors.

The most persuasive words of the debate were spoken by two men: Randolph, who, as we have seen, had strong convictions against paper money, and George Mason, who was similarly disposed. Despite their feelings, they struck out against the prohibition, begging the delegates not to tie the hands of Congress in unforeseen emergencies. The upshot of the debate was an action that seemed to be all things to all men. On one hand, the authority of Congress to issue bills of credit was struck from the draft. Yet, on the other, the delegates were doubtless moved by the prophetic words of Randolph and Mason and could not bring themselves to outlaw paper money. In any event no action was taken on the proposed prohibition, and the truncated clause authorizing coinage alone (the present Article I, Section 8, Clause 5) was adopted.

On August 28 the question of money power returned to the floor with a reverse twist. This time, debate was on the drafting committee's proposal to bar states from coining money without congressional consent. Two delegates moved that the prohibition be extended to emitting bills of credit and to making anything but gold and silver coin a legal tender. They also suggested that all these bars be made absolute, instead of revocable at the direction of Congress. This provision, so amended, passed easily, with the concluding remark that such action was the "favorable crisis for crushing paper money."

Indicative, however, of the fact that legal tender is but a means to a larger end was a proposal that followed immediately in a suggestion to forbid newly admitted states from interfering in private contracts. After considerable wrangling, this was changed and passed as a measure forbidding newly admitted states from divesting private rights through bills of attainder (that is, legislative trials) and "retrospective laws." [11]

Both provisions then seemed to get lost in the process of drafting, but their substance (Article I, Section 10, Clause 1, as set out in the chapter headnote) was added as an amendment to the final document on September 14. Significantly, when this provision was inserted, the Convention rejected a proposal to forbid congressional impairment of contracts and, thereby, maintained a position consistent with its decision on legal tender. That is, although authority was not specifically given, a proposal to deny the power was rejected.

Only one further debate of the Convention need detain us, and it also took place on September 14 in connection with an abortive proposal to empower Congress to provide for a system of canals. Madison suggested the proposed authority be enlarged to "grant charters of incorporation when the interest of the United States might be required and the legislative provisions of the States may be incompetent." The proposed amendment failed for contradictory reasons. One delegate said spelling out the power to create corporations was unnecessary and even dangerous, since it might be used to establish a bank, "a subject of contention." [12] Another delegate joined the opposition but for precisely the opposite reason;

[11] *Documents Illustrative of the Formation of the Union of the American States,* p. 628.
[12] Id., p. 724.

he felt that the power of incorporation was not implied, and, if specified, might be used to promote monopolies.

It was upon this sparse collection of words that the monetary deliberations of the Convention closed. But what about our experts? Unfortunately, their counsel was lost through the combination of the infirmity of age and the rashness of youth. The heat of the summer and the weight of Franklin's eighty-two years combined to keep his appearances in debate to a minimum. This was a real loss, for his views on paper money—which he had both printed on his press and defended with his pen—would have been most cogent. Hamilton, on the other hand, was youthful, vigorous, and still working out his ideas on a national bank, which he felt offered the key to expansion without inflation. However, his influence at the Convention was shattered by a speech of June 18, when he plumped for the strongest of central governments and managed to outrage friend and enemy alike by a florid endorsement of the British monarchy.

Certain decisions of the Convention are clear enough. Obviously, Congress can mint coin and establish its value. The states cannot. Neither can the states issue currency of the colonial type. The legal tender powers of states affect only forms of money they cannot issue. But there were other questions that were not answered. What about banks which issued their own notes? Could Congress charter one? Could it control those chartered by the states? Could Congress put out a paper money? Could it make it a legal tender? What was the relationship between monetary authority of Congress and its seemingly unrestricted borrowing power? These questions were among the ones the late Justice Robert H. Jackson described as being "so delicate that the framers would have risked their unity if an answer had been forced . . . they knew that to get acceptance of [the Constitution's] fundamental design for government many controversial details were left to be filled in from time to time by the wisdom of those who were to follow." [13]

THE NATURE OF CONSTITUTIONAL POWERS

The Congress shall have Power . . . To make all Laws which shall be necessary and proper for carrying into Execution the foregoing Powers, and all other Powers vested by this Constitution in the Government of the United States, or in any Department or Officer thereof.—United States Constitution, Article I, Section 8, Clause 18.

Conventional relationships and accepted ways of doing things change, but the pattern of change varies. The patterns which resulted in the institution of paper money, the winning of political independence, and the adoption of the Constitution, for example, were all different. Some changes were abrupt and dramatic. Some came about gradually and almost imperceptibly. A change of the latter order, which began during the American Revolution and was slowly developing during the Constitutional Convention, was the rise of the commercial bank or, as it was called in the language of those days, the bank of issue. The gradual pattern of change shifted when the adoption of the Constitution gave this new institution a strong forward thrust.

The first American commercial bank was chartered at Philadelphia by the Continental Congress in 1781 as a war finance measure. Other commercial banks were founded shortly thereafter under state charter, one in Boston and another in New York. Although it is true that certain institutions called "banks" had existed in colonial America, these were organizations whose capital and collateral consisted of

[13] Proceedings on the 150th Anniversary of the Supreme Court, 60 S. Ct. CXXXIX.

real estate mortgages and were more fully and accurately denominated "land banks."[14] The new commercial bank counted its basic resource in gold and silver, against which it issued bearer notes payable on demand.

The very assurance of payment implicit in the notes of a responsible issuer, the desperate need for a circulating medium, and the convenience of paper combined to guarantee the issuing bank that presentment of notes for payment would be the exception and not the rule. Herein lay the core of this financial revolution. As long as a commercial bank's note issue was equal to or less than the coin supplied by depositors and stockholders, the bank was only an institution for the safekeeping of coin. The instant it issued notes in excess of such coin—and it could safely do so to the extent notes would not be presented for redemption—it created new money just as if the government had done so at the mint or the printing press. There was, however, one radical difference between these notes and the old state currencies. The commercial bank was a relatively passive instrument in the issuing process. Demand for its notes was produced outside the organization by the requirements of trade and commerce, in sharp distinction to the fiscal needs which dictated the issuance of pre-constitutional paper money.

It was such a note-issuing commercial bank that Alexander Hamilton proposed when, as the first Secretary of the Treasury, he submitted his famous *Report on a National Bank* to Congress in 1791. Although his proposal showed a superficial similarity to contemporary state-chartered organizations, the Bank of England was his real model. Hamilton wanted a truly national organization which would assist the fiscal operations of the government, attract foreign capital, and, by using the gold and silver so obtained in the note expansion

14 Whereas the savings and loan association is considered a Johnny-come-lately to the American financial scene, its functional ancestor, the colonial land bank, actually antedates commercial banks by a good margin.

process, make productive loans and increase the circulating money of the country. Hamilton was convinced that the national circulation would have to be paper and that only a quasi-public corporation operated on business principles could avoid the excesses of earlier times.

A bill to this end was introduced in Congress. It ran into sharp opposition on the grounds that the national government had no power to grant the charter in the absence of a constitutional provision to that effect and that any such Gargantuan organization would be an unrepublican monopoly. The proponents responded that the specified powers were ends, that the Constitution permitted reasonable means to achieve them, and that establishment of corporations was such a means. They repeated and elaborated Hamilton's arguments on the economic feasibility of the bank, and eventually carried the day. The charter passed and went to the President on February 14, 1791.

However, the great debate had just begun. Washington called for the opinions of his Cabinet and thus sparked the first skirmish of the Hamilton-Jefferson controversy that continues to our own day. Jefferson turned in a mild and concise memorandum. He pointed out that Congress possessed only delegated powers, and that the limitations so imposed were fortified by the recently adopted Tenth Amendment. He went on to say that the power of establishing corporations was not specifically delegated, indeed had been voted down at the Convention, and that if it were to be found by implication in the Constitution, could only rest in the clause authorizing Congress to tax and spend for the general welfare, or in the "necessary and proper" clause which concluded the specific grants of congressional power. This, he insisted, could not be; if either clause could be stretched this far, there was no need of any specific grants at all and Congress could do anything it wanted. Then, winding up on a curious note, he suggested that if the pros and cons of constitutionality seemed about equal to the President, the charter might be signed out of respect to the Congress which passed it.

Hamilton did not treat the issue as a polite discussion between Virginia gentlemen, but responded in one of the great state papers of American history. His only concession was made at the beginning in an admission that not one word in the Constitution said or even hinted that Congress could set up corporations. He then went on to expound another truism —that within its explicitly delegated powers the United States was sovereign and had, therefore, the right to employ all reasonable means to give these powers effect. He stated that Congress could not set up a corporation to regulate the police of Philadelphia because it had no jurisdiction over such a subject. On the other hand, he pointed out that it could borrow money, collect taxes, and regulate interstate and foreign commerce. Could it set up a corporation to aid these unquestioned powers?

For his answer he turned to the "necessary and proper" clause (Article I, Section 8, Clause 18) which concluded the specific grants of power, and with suitable underlining drove his point home by asserting that Congress could "make all *Laws* . . . necessary and proper for *carrying into Execution* the foregoing Powers, and all *other Powers* vested by this Constitution in the Government of the United States, or in any *Department* or *Officer* thereof." From this premise he argued that "necessary" did not mean "absolutely or indispensably necessary" but rather "needful, requisite, incidental, useful, or conducive to." He concluded his case by suggesting a criterion to test any proposal presented under this rule of liberal construction: "Does the proposed measure abridge a pre-existing right of any State or of any individual?" [15] Under these standards, the bank went through, and

[15] Richard B. Morris (editor), *Alexander Hamilton and the Founding of the Nation* (New York: The Dial Press, 1957), p. 265.

Washington signed its charter on February 25, 1791.[16]

Let us pause here and note two aspects of the bank controversy. The first is the unique way in which the money power was born. The theory was denied at the door; the accomplished fact was slipped in through the window. This seeming anomaly was in fact a brilliant solution of the bills of credit dilemma inherited from the Constitutional Convention, for it provided at one and the same time a paper money issued under the authority of the United States and a currency free from the control of the political branches of the government. The latter consideration was not articulated in the memorandum to the President, but Hamilton spelled it out clearly enough in his earlier report to Congress where he denounced the direct government issue of currency as a "seducing and dangerous expedient" inconsistent with the spirit of the Constitution.

The second aspect concerns the direction in which this power, once brought into being, would move in achieving its legitimacy. What of the logic by which Hamilton attained his result? We notice that although he brilliantly demonstrated the necessity of implied powers, the very result he desired necessarily confined his thesis to auxiliary, or secondary, powers—as the test of "no trespassing" on state or individual rights plainly showed. Should Congress (to use Hamilton's example) set up a corporation to administer the Philadelphia police, and so trespass on the right of the State of Pennsylvania, it would presumably be brought to heel by the Supreme Court. But a constitutional power is not necessarily secondary or limited merely because it is implied. Indeed, the very act of the Court in ousting Congress from control of the Philadelphia police—on the basis of its authority to overturn the action of every legislature and court in the

16 1 Stat. 191.

land—would be the exercise of an implied power.[17] When power grows to this dimension, it is not secondary but plenary. That is to say, its only restraining check or balance is self-restraint. A plenary power can, of course, be explicit, as is the authority of Congress to declare war when and against whom it pleases. But whether express or implied, the exercise of plenary power cannot be resisted by "a pre-existing right of any State or any individual." To state the matter more exactly, there are no such rights when a plenary power is exercised.

Ironically enough, the legal basis of the transformation of monetary authority from a secondary to a plenary power was foreshadowed by Hamilton himself. After discussing express and implied powers (or, more precisely, implied secondary powers), he went on to say:

> And for the sake of accuracy it shall be mentioned that there is another class of powers, which may be properly denominated resulting powers. It will not be doubted that if the United States should make a conquest of the territories of any of its neighbors, they should possess sovereign jurisdiction over the conquered territory. *This would rather be a result from the whole mass of the powers of the government and from the nature of political society, than a consequence of either of the powers specifically enumerated.* [Italics added.] [18]

Translate "resulting powers" as "implied plenary powers," and the end of the trail is in sight; for, as we shall see, nearly a century later the Supreme Court used different words, but

[17] The Court's power derives from two short phrases in the Constitution: "The judicial Power shall extend to all Cases . . . arising under this Constitution . . ." (Article III, Section 2, Clause 1). And "This Constitution . . . shall be the supreme Law of the Land . . ." (Article VI, Clause 2). As a practical matter, it is also based on the undeniable fact of life that, in an orderly society, argument has to stop somewhere.
[18] Morris, p. 264.

precisely the same idea, to validate the money power in its full magnitude.[19]

[19] We might note a third aspect of the Jefferson-Hamilton bank controversy and that is the use of constitutional theory as a device of tactical opposition. Constitutional theories have, of course, a vitality and significance of their own. Yet the power and responsibility of the national government in general, and the presidency in particular, permit certain *general* doctrines being asserted as an initial line of defense against a *specific* measure or program. Thus, the canons of strict construction of the Constitution, states' rights, the independence of Congress and/or of the courts, can be readily asserted against almost any program in which the Executive would be involved. As we know, Jefferson, the President, did not let strict construction bar his acquisition of the Louisiana Territory or (of more serious constitutional doubt) his commitment to grant American citizenship to all French nationals in that area.

II

The nation and the states

The powers not delegated to the United States by the Constitution, nor prohibited by it to the States, are reserved to the States respectively, or to the people.—Tenth Amendment to the Constitution of the United States.

When the Constitution put the states out of the money business, it gave commercial banking a tremendous lift. The three state-chartered banks of 1784 grew to eighty-eight by 1800. We have seen that these institutions, by issuing bank notes, were creators of money, and that this power was limited only by the necessity of keeping enough coin in their tills to cover the notes presented for redemption. However, the banking policy of the time was generally conservative, and the issue of notes was not pressed to anything near the limit.

This salutary convention was also observed by the new federal bank.[1] The Bank of the United States was a "quasi-

[1] The official title of both this institution and its successor was "The President, Directors, and Company, of the Bank of the United States." In the early nineteenth century they were known as the "national" banks, a term we presently

public" corporation. "Quasi-private" would perhaps be a better term. The national government owned 20 per cent of the $10 million stock and appointed five of twenty-five directors; and the federal bank in turn handled the government's deposits, transferred its funds, and assisted in its financing. The bulk of the bank's operations were those of a well-run, profit-minded business, and necessarily so, since the bank got no revenue from the government, but was expected to pay its own way.

The bank's loan policies enabled it to restrain the note issue activities of the state-chartered commercial banks. The federal bank made short-term commercial loans. Repayments by borrowers, as well as general business activities, brought in considerable sums in notes issued by the state banks. The federal bank did not pay out such notes again, but sent them to the issuing banks for redemption. If the issuing institution did not have enough federal bank notes to cover, the difference had to be made up in coin. This put a ceiling over state bank note issue, and like other instruments of monetary policy, its origin was not premeditated, but accidental. Note redemption produced no real difficulty at this time, since the federal bank was tactful in demands, and state banks observed conservative issue margins.

Yet, as early as 1807, the federal bank got an omen of what was in store for it. Georgia laid a tax on the Savannah branch; and when payment was not forthcoming, the state revenue officers simply broke in and took some $2,000 in coin. The bank went to the nearest federal court and sought the

---

ascribe to any commercial bank operating under a federal charter. Conversely, the earlier institutions are often now referred to as the first (or second) Bank of the United States.

Since these early institutions were *central* banks (i.e., organizations whose operations have a purpose transcending private profit and which deal *de jure* or *de facto* with "retail" banks as the monetary arm of government), Bray Hammond has used "federal bank" to describe them in his *Banks and Politics in America* (Princeton: Princeton University Press, 1957). His convention is followed here.

return of its money. It gained a temporary victory, which was reversed by the Supreme Court on the ground that the bank had no authority to sue where it did and, instead, should have sought the protection of the Georgia courts.[2]

By the time the federal bank's charter came up for renewal in 1811, adversities closed in on it. The practice of redeeming state bank notes had stirred up some opposition. Jeffersonian tradition, in which hatred of the federal bank was an article of faith, was running at flood tide. Perhaps most important of all, Anglo-American relations were rapidly deteriorating. Hamilton's plan for attracting foreign capital had succeeded too well, for 70 per cent of the federal bank's stock was in foreign, largely British, hands. Stock held by foreigners was nonvoting; hence the contention of some of the bank's opponents that, on the eve of the War with England, the nation's financial citadel was dominated by the enemy was untrue. But it was true that the greater part of the bank's dividends went to foreigners and that this constituted a heavy drain on the nation's gold and silver coin. For these several reasons Congress rejected the charter renewal, and the first federal bank came to an end on February 25, 1811.

This dissolution gave state banking a powerful impetus. The outbreak of the War of 1812 provided another, as the government turned to state-chartered institutions for help in war financing. Between 1811 and 1815, the number of state banks jumped from eighty-eight to two hundred and forty-six. The tremendous increase in banks of issue, the return of

[2] *Bank of the United States* v. *Deveaux* (1809), 9 U.S. (5 Cranch), 61. Generally speaking, the lower federal courts can take cases: (1) on the basis of the parties, i.e., suits between *citizens* of different states, and (2) on the basis of the controversy, i.e., if a federal law or the Constitution is involved. The Deveaux case turned on whether a corporation was a "citizen," and tentatively established the doctrine that if all stockholders were citizens of the same state (obviously not so in the case of the first federal bank), they could be collectively associated under the corporate name to establish the requisite diversity of citizenship.

$7 million in gold to Europe, and the dislocations caused by the war finally undermined the convertibility of the American bank note currency. In 1814 most state banks "suspended" specie payments, that is, refused to pay their notes in coin.[3] This removed the built-in governor which had previously limited the amount of note issues; and the rise in the number of state banks was paralleled by an expansion in their note issue from $22 to $68 million.

This deluge of paper compounded the troubles of a three-year war, not only because of its inflationary action but also because of its inability to replace the notes of the first federal bank as a national currency. Congress finally settled the question of its power to issue paper money by authorizing successive wartime issues of Treasury notes, issued in theory as government securities but in large practical measure as money.[4] Such action, however, only accelerated the price rocketing. All in all, monetary institutions slipped back to the pre-constitutional slough, and then some; for the thirteen local currencies of 1787 had by 1816 run to over two hundred. The pre-constitutional paper made at least a pretense of passing within state borders, but the state bank notes were parochial creatures with a very limited mobility. The further they went from the issuing bank, the more they were discounted. Moreover, the discounts were not based

---

[3] Suspension of specie payments by a single bank was its flag of surrender, marking a confession of the failure of individual management. However, a general suspension of specie payments—in a city, state, or throughout the nation—was a fundamentally different matter, being the melancholy manifestation of war, economic collapse, or other general adversity. Such mass suspension was the spontaneous and unorganized, but nonetheless effective, banking response when too many people wanted specie (gold and silver coin). The banks simply stopped paying specie out, but otherwise continued business as usual. State legislatures recognized the difference between the two types of suspensions, for laws placing severe penalties on a bank's failure to redeem bank notes in specie were often suspended or repealed upon the occurrence of a collective bank failure to do so.

[4] 2 Stat. 766; 2 Stat. 801; 3 Stat. 100; 3 Stat. 161; 3 Stat. 213.

solely on distance. Banks were often hastily founded and imprudently operated.

Doubtless, these free and easy conditions reflected the ebullient impulses that were turning the country from Federalist conservatism to Jeffersonian democracy, but the apprehension of mismanagement and failure often showed up in the limited local acceptance of notes. The crazy-quilt money situation made travel difficult, impeded transfers of funds, restricted trade and commerce, and severely handicapped Treasury operations. Jeffersonian tradition finally yielded to the logic of facts. President Madison, who had assailed the constitutionality of the first federal bank during the congressional debates on its charter, asked for the establishment of a second federal bank in his outgoing State of the Union message. His successor, James Monroe, signed the revived institution's charter on April 10, 1816.[5]

Correction of the deranged currency had been stressed over and over again in proposals for the second federal bank. The tactics the bank had to use were fairly obvious—first, get the state banks back on a basis of redeeming their notes in specie and, second, keep the amount of their issues within limits by presenting notes for redemption or refusing to accept them for taxes when the issues became excessive. This was more easily said than done. The country was losing gold to England as imports exceeded exports. The postwar surge of development and expansion was putting pressure on the banking system for loans. The overwhelming number of state banks had come into being when the old practice of keeping an ample supply of specie to cover outstanding notes was as outdated as the powdered wigs of the Philadelphians who originated the convention. The only way the new state banks could possibly keep their notes redeemable in specie was to restrict their note issues and hence to curtail the lending facilities available to their communities. Local hostility to

[5] 3 Stat. 266.

the federal bank resulting from such loss of credit was fortified by a continuous apprehension on the part of local bank
customers that the federal bank might make good on its
threats of forced redemption and nonacceptance of the notes
of overissued local banks. These contingencies were a persistent menace to any local bank and could well cause the
local banker's sins to be visited on the heads of the whole
community. Moreover, the second federal bank was badly,
even scandalously, managed at the outset of its career and
was in no position to assume the role of guarding monetary
probity. Hence, a rash of retaliatory state legislation erupted.

The second federal bank, like its predecessor, received no
income from the government, but depended for revenue on
its private lending operation. The state enactments struck at
this financial jugular by laying a tax on the federal bank's
notes or, in practical effect, on its loans. A 10 per cent tax
meant the federal bank had to raise its interest rate equiva-
lently if it did not want to lose money, but the very act of
raising its rate to such levels put it out of competition as a
lender. These acts did not refer to the federal bank by name,
but theoretically applied to all banking institutions in the
enacting state that were not chartered by it. They were cast
in the form of conventional revenue measures. Despite their
innocent surface, everyone understood their origin and purpose.

THE FALSE DAWN OF FEDERAL SUPREMACY

A man named James McCulloch was cashier of the Baltimore
branch of the federal bank, and while holding that office,
had several brushes with the law. The first infraction as-
sured, if not his place in American history, at least the per-
manency of his name as long as that history is taught. His
supposed offense lay in putting untaxed notes into circula-

tion. He was haled into court through an informer's suit.
The Baltimore County Court returned a judgment against
him, and its decision was affirmed by the highest tribunal of
Maryland. McCulloch appealed to the Supreme Court, and
the legal battle of the century was on.

Daniel Webster, counsel for the second federal bank, and
Luther Martin, an inflationist *enfant terrible* of the Constitutional Convention and now the Maryland Attorney General,
rehashed at tedious length the arguments exchanged a generation earlier when the first federal bank was successively
praised and cursed through Congress and the Cabinet. They
dug up a few new ones based on the Maryland tax. Martin
invoked the shade of an old enemy and the spiritual father
of the bank by quoting Hamilton's statement in the thirty-
second Federalist Paper that save for the prohibited tax on
exports and imports, the Constitution left states with "an independent and uncontrollable authority to raise their own
revenue . . . in the most absolute and unqualified sense."
Webster countered with the grim axiom that "an unlimited
power to tax is the power to destroy."

John Marshall presided over the Supreme Court as its
fourth Chief Justice. He had dourly observed the state bank
excesses of the postwar boom, and found them offensive both
to his conservative economic prepossession and to his strong
nationalist bent. Statesman rather than judge, he saw more
in the shabby informer's suit than a revolt of the backwoods
against the money center, and more than a state's questionable attempt to check a questionable federal power. Rather,
he appraised the litigation as the juncture at which the am-
biguities, silences, and generalities of the Constitutional Convention could no longer compose the latent conflict of state
and nation, and at which the country had a choice of two
roads: one back to the weak confederacy of the Articles; the
other forward to a United States. He gave it a firm shove
down the second road, and it has never looked back.

Marshall spoke for a unanimous Court and reversed the Maryland judgment. His opinion, the longest he ever wrote, covers some thirty-three closely printed pages. We can extract its core with four quotations. The first set at rest once and for all the question of whether Congress had only the specific powers enumerated in the Constitution or whether these were ends in themselves to be achieved by the use of additional means by reason of the "necessary and proper" clause. Following Hamilton's lead, and at times copying him verbatim, Marshall took the word "necessary" and expounded it in a brilliant tour de force that resolved half of the issues of the case:

> . . . Does it always import an absolute physical necessity so strong that one thing, to which another may be termed necessary, cannot exist without that other? We think it does not . . . we find that it frequently imports no more than that one thing is convenient, or useful, or essential to another. . . . This word, then, like others, is used in various senses; and, in its construction, the subject, the context, the intention . . . are all to be taken into view. . . . Let this be done in the case under consideration. The subject is the execution of those great powers on which the welfare of a nation essentially depends. It must have been the intention of those who gave these powers, to insure . . . their beneficial execution. This could not be done by confining the choice of means to . . . narrow limits. . . . This provision is made in a constitution intended to endure for ages to come, and, consequently, to be adapted to various crises of human affairs.[6]

The Chief Justice propounded this generality against the following particulars:

> . . . Throughout this vast republic, from the St. Croix to the Gulf of Mexico, from the Atlantic to the Pacific,

6 McCulloch v. Maryland (1819), 17 U.S. (4 Wheaton), 316, 413.

revenue is to be collected and expended, armies are to be marched and supported. The exigencies of the nation may require that the treasure raised in the north should be transported to the south, that raised in the east conveyed to the west, or that this order should be reversed. Is that construction of the constitution to be preferred which would render these operations difficult, hazardous, and expensive? [7]

The question, of course, answered itself and Marshall upheld the bank as a legitimate exercise of federal authority in a ringing declaration:

. . . Let the end be legitimate, let it be within the scope of the constitution, and all means are appropriate, which are plainly adapted to that end, which are not prohibited, but consist with the letter and spirit of the constitution, are constitutional. [8]

Marshall could not follow Hamilton too far, since the latter, as we have seen, had expressly conceded the right of a state to misuse its "absolute" tax powers. Hence, the Chief Justice adroitly shifted authorities, picked up Webster's argument that "the power to tax is the power to destroy," and pronounced the Maryland levy unconstitutional:

If the states may tax one instrument, employed by the government in the execution of its powers, they may tax any and every other instrument. They may tax the mail; they may tax the mint; they may tax patent-rights; they may tax the papers of the customhouse; they may tax judicial process; they may tax all the means employed by the government, to an excess which would defeat all the ends of government. [9]

[7] *Id.*, 17 U.S. (4 Wheaton), 316, 408.
[8] *Id.*, 17 U.S. (4 Wheaton), 316, 421.
[9] *Id.*, 17 U.S. (4 Wheaton), 316, 432.

The foregoing quotations rank among the most important judicial writing in history, for they are canons of constitutional law second in importance only to the Constitution itself. Yet insofar as the real issues are concerned, the opinion is inadequate; for it says a great deal about the power of the United States in general and nothing whatever about the monetary authority of the United States in particular.

Indeed, like Hamilton's earlier polemics, it stays as far away as possible from theorizing on the money power as such. Note what constitutional provisions it cites in justifying the bank: the taxing power, the spending power, and the war power. On the other hand, it does not even mention Congress' specific power to coin and regulate the value of money,[10] nor any implicit power the government may have to this end. It does not mention the prime purpose for which the federal bank was chartered, to bring order out of the chaos of state bank notes. It does not mention the attempt to do this by a combination of force and cajolery. Even Maryland's tax, which had no other purpose than to expel a hated intruder from its borders, is blandly treated as a run-of-the-mill revenue measure. At best we can appraise the significance of the case as being the first breach of Hamilton's test. If the states had any pre-existing right to lay a discriminatory tax on any federal activity (monetary or otherwise) before the McCulloch case, assuredly they had none after it.[11]

[10] The first appraisal of the "coin and regulate" clause in a Supreme Court opinion seems to be in *U.S. v. Marigold* (1850), 50 U.S. (8 Howard), 560, a counterfeiting case.

[11] Parts of the opinion written in Marshall's "all or nothing" style would seem to indicate that *any* state tax on any federal activity was unconstitutional. However, the *discriminatory* impact of the Maryland tax was its fatal flaw; for in closing, Marshall observed: "[This opinion] does not extend to a tax paid by the real property of the bank, in common with other real property within the state, nor to a tax imposed on the interest which the citizens of Maryland may hold in this institution, in common with other property of the same description throughout the state," 17 U.S. (4 Wheaton), 316, 437. The reservation furnished the base for state taxation of Federal Reserve banks (38 Stat. 258) and national banks (44 Stat. 1499).

For the specific judicial roots of monetary authority, we must move on to 1824 and the case of *Osborn et al.* v. *The Bank of the United States*.[12] The controversy involved a repressive Ohio tax statute similar to the Maryland one, and began when the state auditor collected the federal bank's delinquent taxes by seizing $100,000 belonging to its Cincinnati branch. The bank went to a federal court, which it was specifically authorized to do under its charter, and got an injunction commanding repayment of the money on the ground that the tax was void. The case went up to the Supreme Court on the narrow technical point of whether Congress could give the federal bank *carte blanche* to sue in a federal court, which it obviously preferred to hostile state judges and juries.[13]

The majority of the Court, speaking through Chief Justice Marshall, held that the federal bank had approached the right tribunal, and restated the McCulloch doctrine of the bank's appropriateness as an instrumentality of the federal government, and its consequent constitutionality and exemption from state taxation. Moreover, the Chief Justice finally got around to mentioning money:

> . . . The currency which [the bank] circulates, by means of its trade with individuals, is believed to make it a more fit instrument for the purposes of government than it could otherwise be. . . .[14]

---

[12] 22 U.S. (9 Wheaton), 738.

[13] As we have seen, unless the parties are citizens of different states, lower federal courts can hear a case only if a federal law is involved. The Osborn case involved the question of whether Congress could make the incident of getting into court the subject of a law, even if the subject of controversy was based on state legislation. The majority held Congress could, and one of the current fruits of the decision is Section 25 of the Federal Reserve Act granting Reserve Banks free access to federal courts.

[14] *Osborn et al.* v. *The Bank of the United States* (1824), 22 U.S. (9 Wheaton), 738, 864.

Significantly, however, this sentence appeared in a part of the opinion which justified the federal bank's commercial activity as aiding and, therefore, not contradicting, its governmental functions. It has no reference whatever to the activity of the bank in attempting to restore monetary stability.

However, one Justice, William Johnson of South Carolina, refused to join the opinion of the Court, and it is his lone dissent that contains the first explicit reference in a Supreme Court opinion to the monetary authority of the national government. We can bypass his reasons why the bank should have gone to an Ohio court, and concentrate instead on the sentence with which he concluded a precise historical account of the monetary debacle of 1812–1815:

> A specie-paying bank, with an overwhelming capital, and the whole aid of the government deposits, presented the only resource to which the government could resort *to restore that power over the currency of the country, which the framers of the constitution evidently intended to give to Congress alone.* [Italics added.] [15]

What was this "power over the currency," so flatly asserted by Justice Johnson? What were its limits, and where did it come from? The mere mention of its existence stands out in contrast to Marshall's persistent refusal to recognize the federal bank's monetary activities and his continuing rationalization of it as a once-removed and almost accidental by-product of a basic congressional authority.

Johnson's view of the matter could have settled the issue summarily, and indeed was to prevail in the long run. How-

[15] *Id.*, 22 U.S. (9 Wheaton), 738, 783. William Johnson (1772–1834) is the forgotten man of American jurisprudence. He was the only Jeffersonian appointee to the Supreme Court to resist Marshall's compelling influence and went his lonely way as "the first dissenter." His opinions have an astonishingly modern ring, for he refused to adopt Marshall's categorical logic and saw most questions as involving difficult problems of degree. Many of the concepts he advanced in his years on the Court (1804–1834) have been incorporated into settled constitutional doctrine but without credit to him.

ever, it was Marshall's roundabout reasoning that carried the day. It was a type of reasoning, however, that was not a settlement of argument, but an invitation to debate. Words like "appropriate" never prove themselves; that something is "appropriate" will be self-evident to some men—because it can be evident in no other way—and will be self-evidently irrational and absurd to others. Indeed, Marshall's criterion of "appropriateness" was to furnish a formal excuse for the extinction of the second bank as a federal corporation.

In 1828, four years after the Osborn decision, Andrew Jackson was elected President. Perhaps governed by an intuitive distrust of the Midas-like ability of a banker to parlay a small amount of coin into a large amount of notes and perhaps embittered by a youthful experience with some worthless notes, Jackson hated all banks. He considered them devices by which knaves flimflammed honest men,[16] and hated the federal bank most because it was the biggest. In his Cabinet there was one man who abhorred the federal bank even more than the President. Roger B. Taney, the Attorney General, had lost a private lawsuit against it that he should have won and thereafter sought its downfall with an unremitting tenacity.

Together (and there is some question as to which of the two was the motivating spirit) they headed up a fantastic coalition, whose only bond was opposition to the second bank. The coalition included "hard money" frontier interests (who felt the note-issue function was intrinsically evil), New York financiers (who wanted the country's financial center

[16] The tenacious tradition that Jackson led "cheap money" agrarians to victory over "high interest" creditors should be classed with the fable of Washington and the cherry tree. The agrarian-frontier philosophy at that time was "hard money" above all. It viewed the note-expansion function of commercial banking with suspicion, and many frontier states actually wrote prohibitions of banking into their constitutions. The same instinctive distaste for a presumed "something-for-nothing" financial device goes far back in history. It doubtless underlay Aristotle's indictment of interest, whereby coin multiplied itself without effort on the part of the owners.

moved from Philadelphia, the headquarters of the second bank, to Manhattan's Wall Street), and, most important, the state-chartered banks who felt the regulatory hand of the federal bank as an intolerable restraint in the exuberant spirit of the day.

The coalition smashed the bank in two steps. The first was the veto of a renewal of its charter; the second was the withdrawal of the government's account and termination of its fiscal agency. Roger Taney contributed mightily to both steps. As Attorney General, he wrote the veto message, and moving up to head of the Treasury, he closed out the government's balances and distributed them among state banks. His reward was the Chief Justiceship of the United States in 1836.

The veto message was a remarkable document, presenting every antibank argument that had been advanced since Jefferson turned in his memorandum to Washington. It trumpeted defiance at the Supreme Court's validation of the federal bank by insisting that institution was nonetheless unconstitutional. It then went on in an attempt to hoist Marshall on his own petard of "appropriateness"—if that were to be the criterion of constitutionality—by an inflammatory indictment of the bank's wealth, power, and lack of political responsibility, which it summed up in the phrase: "Advancement of the few at the expense of the many."

The bank's case could not withstand the savage rhetoric. Arguments that inflationary ravages had been moderated, that the country had a dependable national currency (and indeed would not get another for almost a century), that the intricacies of foreign exchange were smoothly handled, were but chaff swept before the wind. The veto held and was ratified by the election of 1832. Thus was the monetary authority of the United States utterly undone by the President, who fiercely asserted the supremacy of the national power in all other actions of his administration.

Yet the Marshall test of the "appropriateness" of a national bank—and the consequent constitutionality of such an institution—sparked debate up to the Civil War. President Tyler adopted Jackson's conclusion of "inappropriateness" in vetoing the charter of a proposed third institution (although, curiously enough, he had left the Democratic party over Jackson's withdrawal of the government's deposit). On the other side of the coin, Lincoln summed up his first platform as ". . . short and sweet like an old woman's dance. I am in favor of a national bank . . . and a high protective tariff."[17] And the feasibility of such an institution was one of the first subjects he debated with Douglas.

The year 1819 was marked not only by the McCulloch decision but also by the end of a postwar boom. The foreign market for staples broke, prices fell, and a wave of business and bank failures engulfed the country. The west and south were doubly beset by disaster because of their dependence on agriculture and the practice of their banks in stretching credits to the breaking point. The result was an almost complete collapse of banking facilities in these areas, which in turn compelled ameliorating state legislation. Two such laws, both passed in 1820, wound up in the Supreme Court.

Missouri had enacted a statute setting up state loan offices to extend credit in the form of "loan certificates." These negotiable, small-denomination, interest-bearing instruments were an ingenious combination of old and new. The credit of the state was placed behind them, they were acceptable for taxes, and the salary of state officers was paid in them. Their ultimate security was one of the most primitive of money substitutes: salt from the state-owned mines. In due course, two borrowers who had applied at a state loan office and had given their note in return for loan certificates, refused to repay. Their refusal was based on the assertion that the certificates they had received (and spent) were state

17 Edgar Lee Masters, *Lincoln the Man* (New York: Dodd Mead and Company, 1931), p. 31.

"bills of credit," outlawed by the Constitution, and that their note, being based on an illegal consideration, was absolutely void. The Missouri courts, unimpressed by the debtors' attempt to eat their cake and have it too, held the debt valid. The case went to the Supreme Court in 1830 under the title *Craig* v. *Missouri*.[18]

It has been noted how the Constitutional Convention handled the question of monetary authority in two steps. On one hand, Congress was vested with certain penumbral powers; on the other, the states were deprived of rights they previously held in this field. The Craig case seemed to complete something of a judicial parallel; for the McCulloch decision had established, albeit cryptically, federal monetary authority, and Craig sharply limited the area of pre-existing state powers when a divided Court pronounced the Missouri law unconstitutional and released the debtors. The Craig opinion follows the style Marshall used so compellingly in McCulloch. First, there is the isolation of a key word, next, a general exposition of the context, and last, a reduction of the generality to particulars. In McCulloch the key was "necessary"; in Craig it was "emit."

Speaking for the majority, the Chief Justice reviewed the provision that "no State shall emit bills of credit" and conceded at the outset that the prohibition could not affect the right of states to borrow and, hence, to issue instruments payable in the future. However, he asserted that the word "emit" when combined with "bills of credit" comprehended the entirely different function of "issuing paper intended to circulate through the community for its ordinary purposes as money, which paper is redeemable at a future day." [19] After reviewing the disastrous history of state currency in the preconstitutional period, he observed:

18 29 U.S. (4 Peters), 410.
19 *Craig* v. *Missouri*, 29 U.S. (4 Peters), 410, 432.

To cut up this mischief by the roots . . . the people declared in their Constitution that no State should emit bills of credit. If the prohibition means anything, if words are not empty sounds, it must comprehend the emission of any paper medium by a State government for the purpose of common circulation.[20]

Turning to the instruments in question and appraising their small denominations and the provision of the authorizing statute for use as tax payments and salaries, he concluded that they were as entirely "bills of credit as if they had been so denominated in the act itself." [21] On these premises it followed that any contract based on a loan of such instruments was the tainted fruit of a tainted tree.

Three members of the Court dissented. Justice Johnson noted that "the terms 'bills of credit' are in themselves vague and general, and, at the present day, almost dismissed from our language." He agreed that the key question lay in whether the action of Missouri in issuing the certificates "was a loan or an emission of paper money, or perhaps, whether it was not an emission of paper money under the disguise of a loan." After a remarkably acute analysis he concluded that the certificates were "of a truly amphibious character," and that the case being a doubtful one, the Missouri law should be upheld, even though it "does indeed approach as near to a violation of the Constitution as it can well go. . . ." [22] Justice John McLean likewise felt that the majority opinion painted with too broad a brush. He suggested that on the basis of history the definition of bills of credit should be restricted to an instrument issued by a state whose circulation as money was enforced by statutes providing for, or approaching, legal tender. However, most pertinent to our

---

[20] *Id.*, 29 U.S. (4 Peters), 410, 432.
[21] *Id.*, 29 U.S. (4 Peters), 410, 433.
[22] *Id.*, 29 U.S. (4 Peters), 410, 444.

survey was the opinion of Justice Smith Thompson, who sensed the implications of the majority opinion for state banks:

> If these certificates are bills of credit, inhibited by the Constitution, it appears to me difficult to escape the conclusion that all bank notes, issued either by the States, or under their authority and permission, are bills of credit falling within the prohibition.[23]

THE RESURGENCE OF STATE AUTHORITY

Perhaps Justice Thompson's dissent inspired the attack on the Kentucky statute, which was a more sophisticated attempt to meet the monetary crisis than the Missouri law. Kentucky itself issued no instruments, but instead set up a corporation, the Bank of the Commonwealth of Kentucky. The president and directors of the institution were chosen by the legislature, and the bank was declared by law to be the exclusive property of the state. The bank had authority to receive deposits, to make loans, and to issue bank notes in the usual form.

In 1831 four co-makers on a note, which had been given for bank notes, refused to repay. The Constitution, it seems, was fast becoming the last refuge of a debtor, for the delinquents argued that their debt to the bank was voided by the supreme law of the land. They advanced the theory that since the prohibition of bills of credit forbade a state to issue paper, it was of no consequence whether such action was attempted directly or through a state-chartered enterprise. The Kentucky courts were unimpressed, and their judgment was appealed to the Supreme Court.

The case was first argued in 1835, when the Court lacked

[23] *Id.*, 29 U.S. (4 Peters), 410, 449.

its full complement due to the resignation of Justice Gabriel Duval. Although a bare majority of the incumbent Justices felt the case was ruled by the Craig decision, they refused to consider a constitutional question without a complete membership.[24] The ranks of the incumbents were further thinned by the death of Chief Justice Marshall in his seventy-ninth year on July 6, 1835. When the matter was reargued in 1837, it was before a Court every member of which, save two, was an appointee of Andrew Jackson. The Court upheld the Kentucky law, Justice McLean writing the majority opinion.

Justice McLean did not attempt to reverse the Craig decision outright, but ostentatiously went out of his way to support it. However, he found two new and distinct questions in the present controversy: first, whether a state could charter a note-issuing bank, and, second, whether it could control such an institution through stock ownership. He answered both affirmatively. As to the first, he pointed out that states had granted charters to banks and other corporations both before and after the adoption of the Constitution, that there was no specific limit in that document on the exercise of such power, and that by their very nature state bank notes could not be struck down as state bills of credit since (and here he eviscerated the Craig decision) "to constitute a bill of credit within the Constitution, it must be issued by a State, on the faith of the State, and be designed to circulate as money." [25] Using this yardstick, he found that the challenged notes were issued neither by Kentucky nor on its credit, but rather by and on the credit of a separate corporate entity. He then quickly disposed of the second question by citing one of Marshall's ideas that a state did not, by becoming a corporator, identify itself with the created corporation. Since it was admitted that a state could thus own stock in a private corporation, Justice McLean could conclude by Marshall's

24 *Briscoe* v. *Bank of Kentucky*, 34 U.S. (9 Peters), 85.
25 *Briscoe* v. *Bank of Kentucky* (1837), 36 U.S. (11 Peters), 257, 318.

all-or-nothing logic that no principle prohibited it from own-
ing the whole. Accordingly, he validated the Kentucky law
setting up the Bank of the Commonwealth of Kentucky.

Justice Joseph Story, Marshall's protégé, was the lone dissenter. He reiterated Marshall's thesis that the constitutional
prohibition of bills of credit was a prohibition of things, not
of words. He pointed out that the bank corporation involved
in the suit was "the sole and exclusive instrument of the
State, managing its exclusive funds, for its exclusive benefit
and under its exclusive management." [26] He accordingly protested that its circulating bank notes were state bills of credit
and, therefore, forbidden. However, the most interesting portion of his dissent tacked a prophetic qualification on the
majority's endorsement of state-chartered banks:

> . . . it has been argued that if this bank be unconstitu-
> tional, all State banks founded on private capital are un-
> constitutional. That proposition I utterly deny. . . . The
> States may create banks as well as other corporations, upon
> private capital; and so far as this prohibition [against emit-
> ting bills of credit] may rightfully authorize them to issue
> bank bills or notes as currency; *subject always to the con-*
> *trol of Congress, whose powers extend to the entire regu-*
> *lation of the currency of the country.* [Italics supplied.] [27]

Here we have what seems to be the second explicit reference to the money power stated as a flat and unqualified
assertion in an obscure dissenting opinion.[28] Thereafter,

[26] *Id.*, 36 U.S. (11 Peters), 257, 340.
[27] *Id.*, 36 U.S. (11 Peters), 257, 348.
[28] Story spoke differently of states' rights in his *Commentaries*, where he
quoted approvingly Webster's doctrine "that it is difficult to maintain on the
face of the Constitution itself and independent of long-continued practice,
the doctrine that the states, not being at liberty to coin money, can authorize
the circulation of bank paper, as currency, at all." *Commentaries on the Constitution* (5th ed., Boston: Little, Brown & Co., 1891), p. 60. Perhaps his judicial comment had been forced by the demise of the second federal bank,
which made state banking indispensable.

there are no such references for a generation. The very idea that the national government even possessed such authority was to be buried deeper before it was disinterred. The reason lay partly in the fact that the abstract doctrine of the federal monetary authority had become hopelessly entangled with its concrete manifestation, the federal bank. When monetary questions again were reviewed, they were assessed by a tribunal headed by Roger Taney, the new Chief Justice of the Supreme Court.

Taney's Court relegated the possible existence of federal monetary control to obscurity as early as 1839, when the case of *Bank of Augusta* v. *Earle* was up for decision.[29] This was a complex suit involving the right of a Georgia-chartered bank to buy negotiable paper in Alabama. The trouble started when the bank's Mobile agent bought a New York draft from a businessman named Earle. The New York drawee defaulted, and the bank sued Earle on his endorser's liability. The latter refused to pay, asserting the whole transaction was a nullity since the Bank of Augusta could not do business outside of Georgia and that, in any event, Alabama had specifically forbidden out-of-state banks to operate within its borders. The latter contention was based on a provision of the Alabama constitution which established a state-owned bank (somewhat like the Bank of the Commonwealth of Kentucky) and further provided that the state should be a two-fifths stockholder in any other bank established in its territory.

Chief Justice Taney, speaking for a majority of the Court, rejected these lines of reasoning. As in the Osborn case, the main issues of the suit are outside our survey, and we need not review the basis on which the majority and minority opinions respectively compelled and disapproved Earle's payment of the draft. In deciding that Alabama law had not prohibited the purchase of the disputed draft, Taney stated:

[29] 38 U.S. (13 Peters), 519.

"The institutions of Alabama . . . are founded upon the great principles of the common law; and it is very clear that at common law, the right of banking in all its ramifications, belonged to individual citizens, and might be exercised by them at their pleasure. . . . Undoubtedly, the sovereign authority might regulate and restrain this right. . . ." What was the "sovereign authority" possessing such power? The Chief Justice made it exceedingly clear that it was not the federal government but the states. For in the selfsame sentence and paragraph he continued, ". . . the constitution of Alabama purports to be nothing more than a restriction upon the power of the Legislature. . . . We are fully satisfied that the State never intended . . . to interfere with the right of purchasing or selling bills of exchange. . . ." [30]

The lone dissenter was Justice John McKinley, but he too joined in the overthrow of the Craig doctrine with his frank reference to Alabama's "performing her duty . . . by providing a circulating medium for the citizens. . . ." [31] The dissent included an unwitting prophecy. Counsel for the debtor argued that the right of Congress to regulate interstate commerce deprived Alabama of any power over an interstate bill of exchange. The entire Court rejected the argument, but only Justice McKinley chose to respond to it:

"If ever Congress shall exercise this power to the broad extent contended for, the power of the States over commerce . . . will be reduced to very narrow limits. *The creation of banks, the making and endorsing of bills of exchange and promissory notes, and the damages on bills of exchange, all relate, more or less, to the commerce among the several States.*" [Italics supplied.] [32]

[30] *Bank of Augusta* v. *Earle* (1839), 38 U.S. (13 Peters), 519, 595.
[31] *Id.*, 38 U.S. (13 Peters), 519, 603.
[32] *Id.*, 38 U.S. (13 Peters), 519, 600.

THE TRIUMPH OF FEDERAL POWER

Justice McKinley's insight into the close connection of banking and interstate commerce was acute, but the legal consequences of this relationship were almost a century away. As far as 1839 was concerned, the states' money power was at the crest of the wave. Its concrete opponent, the second federal bank, had been struck down some years previously, and the constitutional bases of its own existence had been given a rousing validation in the Briscoe and Bank of Augusta decisions.

Yet in this very year the eclipse of state authority was being prefigured in a New York banking development which involved securing bank notes by a deposit of public bonds. The anchoring of bank notes to such securities rather than to specie was intended to avoid the difficulties that dependence on coin persistently entailed, and at the same time to provide a note issue that was both secured in value and limited in amount.[33]

This New York plan provoked much favorable comment, and suggestions were made that it be adopted on a national scale. Actually, the very breadth of discussion of the banking and currency situation plainly showed that the seeming golden age of state banking was fading. The currency situation left much to be desired. State banks were growing by leaps and bounds. There were over eight hundred in 1839,

[33] We should also note for the record the historic Louisiana Banking Act of 1842, which required a one third gold reserve against notes *and* deposits and prefigured Federal Reserve legislation in provisions for: (1) commercial paper backing of other notes and deposits, (2) periodic state examinations, and (3) regular publication of bank statements. However, in our context the New York development was far more significant: "The Louisiana Act confined banks to the provision of bank credit for short-term monetary purposes. . . . The New York Act took the bold step of resting the value of money on political authority; and opened the way to the relegation of gold to a mystical arcanum where the State is absolute and the individual never enters to touch the precious stuff." Hammond, p. 680.

and they had doubled in number by the time the Civil War broke out. This growth both shaped and reflected a tremendous surge in national economic growth. Indeed, economic growth could not have taken place without the state banks. Yet there was a price to be paid. Every new state bank added to the incredible variety of bank notes in circulation. Some were notes good as gold; some were not worth the paper they were printed on. Most were in between, and practically all circulated at varying rates of discount. This vexing condition produced an increasing demand for a currency that would be worth a hundred cents on the dollar in both New Orleans and Boston.

The demand was reflected in the 1856 inaugural address of the Governor of Ohio, who reviewed the pressing need for an adequate national currency and concluded that the states were unable to do the job: "Such a currency, however, is only attainable through the legislation of Congress and the action of the General Government."[34] The speaker's name was Salmon P. Chase, and in 1861 he became Lincoln's Secretary of the Treasury.

Chase inherited an empty till, a plummeting national credit, and unprecedented demands for money. His burden was complicated by the general preoccupation with military affairs, by his optimistic forecast of the length of the war, and by his assumption that he knew something about finance (Chase had served as Ohio counsel for the federal bank). When his initial bond issues were less than successful, he came up with the idea of financing the war and reforming the currency by the single stroke of putting every bank still in the Union on the New York "safety fund" system. The bonds in such a fund would, of course, be federal issues. In December of 1861 his recommendation for this project went to the House Ways and Means Committee. The committee

[34] *The Origin of the National Banking System* (Senate Document No. 582, 61st Congress, 2d Session, 1910), p. 31.

ignored it, and reported out a bill proposing a $150 million issue of Treasury notes, to be in small denominations, without interest, and to be a legal tender. This was the last thing Chase wanted, and he had expressed his "grave aversion" about such paper in previous correspondence to the Ways and Means Committee.

The whole "legal tender" story lies ahead of us. At this point it need only be noted that Chase finally secured congressional action on his banking plan the following year, and Lincoln signed the first National Bank Act (12 Stat. 680) on February 25, 1863, seventy-two years to the day after Washington approved the charter of the first federal bank. Under this law any five or more persons could form a bank by raising the required capital, filing their papers with the Treasury, and buying the required amount of government bonds.[35] The bonds were then deposited with the Treasury, and engraved notes equal to 90 per cent of their par value were returned to the bank. State banks could have the same note-issue privilege by buying the bonds.

Chase assumed that such doubly enhanced capital, drawing interest both from the government bonds and the debts of borrowers, plus certain tax advantages, would bring most banks into the national system. He was wrong. State banks eventually entered in large numbers, but they came in as conscripts. Their entry was compelled by a law which delivered the federal riposte to *McCulloch* v. *Maryland* through a 10 per cent note-issue tax on any bank paying out state bank notes after July 1, 1866.[36] Like the Maryland statute, the tax was intended as a death sentence. Unlike the Maryland law, it produced some quick and drastic results. In

[35] Thus did the federal statute incorporate "free banking" (a concept summed up in Taney's Bank of Augusta reference that "at common law, the right of banking . . . belonged to individual citizens, and might be exercised by them at their pleasure. . . .") and provide a sharp departure from the two earlier federal banking experiments.

[36] 13 Stat. 469. The tax has become a permanent fixture in federal law. Its latest form is §§ 4881–4886 of the Internal Revenue Code of 1954.

1865 alone the number of state banks dropped from 1,089 to 349.

Why was this death sentence passed in the spring of 1865, when the war was practically over and the combined Treasury and national bank notes were doing the job, albeit imperfectly, as a national currency? First of all, the state banks of the north enhanced their fortunes, but not their reputations, during the war. Their continuing squabble with the Treasury over war finance (in which the Treasury was by no means blameless) plus their use of legal tender notes in lieu of conventional gold coin reserves lost them a large measure of public respect. More dangerous to their cause was the sense of nationalism engendered by the Civil War itself,[37] a sentiment which involved three closely related conse‐ quences. One was a feeling that the failure of the federal government to provide a national currency between 1836 and 1861 had given the Confederacy a ready-made appara‐ tus of war finance. Another was a determination that never again would a rebelling state have a banking weapon in its arsenal.[38] Finally, there was the growing realization that commercial banking per se was a governmental function, not because commercial banks took the government's deposits

[37] Usually the law lags behind rather than precedes events in the world of reality, but the constitutional doctrines of Marshall, which provided the legal basis of American nationalism, were ahead of that nationalism, in its substantive sense, by a generation or so. It was the Civil War that, in the movie-maker's phrase, produced the birth of a nation. Men certainly looked at their country and government in a different light before 1860. Examples are Chase's curious reference to "the general government" in his Ohio inaug‐ ural and the chivalrous Lee's attitude that his Virginia birth transcended his soldier's oath. Perhaps a simple grammatical test is the most revealing of all: Up to the Civil War and for a short time subsequently "the United States" is frequently followed in treaties and other like documents by the third person plural; thereafter it is usually followed by the third person singular.

[38] *The Origin of the National Banking System*, pp. 111–112. See also Chief Justice Morrison R. Waite's dissent in *Keith* v. *Clark* (1878), 97 U.S. (7 Otto), 454, 467: "It is an historical fact that the banks of the insurgent States . . . were used extensively in furtherance of the rebellion, and that all or nearly all their available funds were converted in one way or another into Confed‐ erate securities."

or handled its funds, but because they created and issued money itself. Senator John Sherman noted both the civic and economic implications in a speech supporting the tax measure: "A still more important feature of this bill is the section to compel the withdrawal of State bank notes. As the volume of currency affects the price of all commodities, I have no doubt that the amount of such paper money now outstanding adds to the cost of our purchases $500,000,000." [39]

A Maine bank resisted the levy, and its case, *Veazie Bank v. Fenno*, came up before the Supreme Court in 1869.[40] The bank assailed the tax as "direct" and claimed it thereby violated the constitutional requirements of apportionment among the states (Article I, Section 2, Clause 3). Further, it argued that the tax was void as a violation of the Tenth Amendment (reserving undelegated powers to the states or the people) by attempting to tip the federal balance through a perverse use of the tax authority.

Chase was now Chief Justice, and he handed down the majority opinion on December 13, 1869. He found the tax to be indirect; but the implications of this conclusion, if left to stand by itself, would have been completely devastating to the federal system and would have stultified the very purpose of a war, which, in Chase's words, had been fought to vindicate "an indestructible Union of indestructible States." Such a tax would have meant (as Marshall pointed out in the converse situation) that the entire state apparatus existed, not by right, but by the grace of the central government. Therefore, Chase had not only to validate the tax as a tax but also to confine its result. He accordingly polished off the last shred of "any pre-existing right" that the states might have in the area of currency issuance:

[39] Quoted in Walter Wyatt, *Constitutionality of Legislation Providing for a Unified Commercial Banking System* (Nineteenth Annual Report of the Federal Reserve Board, 1932), p. 244.
[40] 75 U.S. (8 Wall.), 533.

. . . it is settled . . . that Congress may constitution-ally authorize the emission of bills of credit . . . there can be no question of the power of the government to emit them . . . to make them a currency, uniform in value and description, and convenient and useful for circulation. These powers, until recently, were only partially and oc-casionally exercised. Lately, however, they have been called into full activity, and Congress has undertaken to supply a currency for the whole country.

Having thus, in the exercise of its undisputed constitu-tional powers, undertaken to provide a currency for the whole country, it cannot be questioned that Congress may, constitutionally, secure the benefit of it to the people. . . . To [this] end, Congress may restrain, by suitable enact-ments, the circulation as money of any notes not issued under its own authority. Without this power, indeed, its attempts to secure a sound and uniform currency for the country must be futile.[41]

Justice Samuel Nelson, dissenting for himself and Justice David Davis, regarded the foregoing questions as far from "settled" and strongly challenged the apodictic tone of the Chief Justice. He pointed out that state banks had been ac-cepted as part of the financial scene for three-quarters of a century and their constitutionality given a resounding en-dorsement in the Briscoe case. He insisted, and correctly, that the tax was not so much an abrogation of the powers of private corporations as it was an unprecedented amputation of state authority. He accordingly rejected the majority opin-ion as finding "no support or countenance in the early history of the government, or in the opinions of the illustrious states-men who founded it." [42]

With the beachhead secured, however, federal monetary authority began to expand with judicial approval into the

[41] *Veazie Bank* v. *Fenno* (1869), 75 U.S. (8 Wall.), 533, 548–549.
[42] *Id.*, 75 U.S. (8 Wall.), 533, 556.

area which historically had been considered the exclusive preserve of state police powers. In 1875 the Court ruled that the powers of a state to protect its citizens from usury simply did not extend to national bank loans.[43] In 1896 the Court refused to apply a New York statute giving preference to certain depositors in an insolvent banking institution, if the latter were a national bank.[44] In 1903 the Court freed a national bank president who had been convicted of violating an Iowa statute forbidding receipt of deposits during insolvency. The Court restated its position on such matters:

> . . . it is not competent for state legislatures to interfere, whether with hostile or friendly intentions, with national banks or their officers in the exercise of the powers bestowed upon them by the general government. . . .[45]

The expansion of federal power continued into the seemingly inviolable sanctuary of the states' equity and probate courts; for in 1913 Congress authorized national banks to become arms of the latter tribunals—that is to say, trustees, executors, and the like—if such activity did not contravene "local law." Congressional action was based on the presumed necessity of keeping national banks on a competitive parity with state institutions engaged in the so-called "trust business." The Attorney General of Michigan challenged the statute, and was upheld by the highest court of that state in a curious ruling which held that although national bank trust activity was consistent with Michigan law, it nonetheless violated the federal Constitution in view of the lack of a "natural" connection between banking and trust business. The Supreme Court held that business practice provided the connection, and, asserting that Congress could legally au-

---

[43] *Farmers' and Mechanics' National Bank* v. *Dearing*, 91 U.S. 29.
[44] *Davis* v. *Elmira Savings Bank*, 161 U.S. 275.
[45] *Easton* v. *Iowa*, 188 U.S. 220, 293.

thorize trust activity, overturned the Michigan judgment.[46] The following year, 1918, Congress endorsed the Court's decision by specifying that trust activity by national banks would not be deemed to violate "local law" if like activity were carried on by state banks and trust companies. This left a question open as to the power of a state to exact safeguards—for example, the deposit of security to protect beneficiaries—which national banks could not meet under their statutory pattern of operations. It was on such ground that a Missouri probate court refused to appoint a national bank as an executor, even though the bank had met the standards of federal law and been nominated by will. The bank eventually took the matter to the Supreme Court and got its appointment in a no-nonsense opinion of Justice Oliver Wendell Holmes that decisively settled matters:

> [The federal statute] says in a roundabout and polite but unmistakable way that whatever may be the State law, national banks . . . may act as executors if trust companies competing with them have that power. The [applicant national bank] has the [federal] permit, competing trust companies can act as executors in Missouri, the importance of the powers to the sustaining of competition in the banking business is so well known and has been explained so fully heretofore that it does not need to be emphasized, and thus the naked question presented is whether Congress had the power to do what it tried to do. . . .
> . . . There is nothing over which a State has more exclusive authority than the jurisdiction of its courts, but it cannot escape its constitutional obligations by the device of denying jurisdiction to courts otherwise competent. . . . So here—the State cannot lay hold of its general control of administration to deprive national banks of their power to compete that Congress is authorized to sustain.[47]

[46] First National Bank v. Union Trust Company (1917), 244 U.S. 416.
[47] State of Missouri v. Duncan (1924), 265 U.S. 17, 23, 24.

THE "POLITE BUT UNMISTAKABLE" SUPERIOR

State monetary authority has shown a remarkable vitality. The interdictions the Constitutional Convention laid on it came to naught because it was tied to an obsolescent form of money, whose replacement by a new monetary institution permitted state money power to rise like Phoenix from the ashes in the form of state-chartered, note-issuing banks. A parallel monetary mutation undid the death sentence tax on state bank notes. Actually, in passing the law, opponents of state banking were beating a dying horse. The bank note, whose utility, in effect, represented an agreement on the part of a number of people to trust the credit of a single organization, was being replaced by another institution of the market place. This new arrival was the check against a deposit in a bank, and its growing use simply meant that the unspoken agreement of trust in the bank was extended by the parties involved to trust in each other. Its net effect was that a bank need not even put out a token substitute in the money-creating process. Now money could be created by the stroke of a pen on a ledger sheet, and the depositor took over distribution of such money by instruments of his own creation.

Just as the constitutional prohibition of bills of credit perversely stimulated the development of a legally acceptable substitute, so did the 10 per cent tax accelerate the inevitable rise of deposit banking. The latter development involved yet another parallel; for just as the remarkable devices of the bill of credit and the bank note broke down again and again when their use was pushed to extremes, the check, valuable and indeed necessary as it was to the financial apparatus of the new industrial era, involved exasperating and often disastrous consequences. Review of the whole tangled and complex problem is far outside our limited scope; however, a limited examination of one facet may both illuminate the whole and set the stage for the litigation that ensued.

We may recall that in the beginnings of note-issue banking a salutary convention was the reservation of an amount of coin to cover the estimated redemptions of notes presented in the course of day-to-day transactions. This convention was brought up to date and given the force of law when state after state, and the federal government as well, made banks chartered under their respective authorities keep cash on hand, the amount fixed as a percentage of deposits. At first this cash "reserve" had to be kept in hand. Later it was permitted to be kept in other banks. The banks selected were, naturally enough, institutions located in cities to which (or through which) funds customarily flowed in the usual course of commerce. Hence, reserves served a double purpose. They satisfied the legal provisions intended to protect depositors. They also provided a "payment fund" at distant points; for when a bank was asked to pay a check drawn on it from a distant city, it did not mail back coin or currency but paid through another check drawn on its reserve depository in that area.

This was a large step forward, since it meant that the rising tide of commercial and industrial activity need not be paralleled by a tremendous amount of currency and coin ceaselessly crossing and recrossing the country. There were, however, drawbacks. Usually the paying bank did not remit one hundred cents on the dollar on a check coming in from out of town. Instead, it deducted a small "exchange charge," which nominally represented its compensation for the money impounded in the out-of-town balance. Actually, the charge involved a modest profit and was passed through the chain of collecting banks and borne by the payee of the check. This diffused the charge over a large number of people—who irritably accepted the modest levy because of the practical difficulty of doing anything else. However, the very existence of exchange charges symbolized the lack of an effective national currency circulating at face value from border to border.

The collection problem had yet another facet. The tremendous number of banks (ten thousand by the turn of the century) operated without any systematic pattern of collections under a catch-as-catch-can "correspondent" system. A bank with an out-of-town check sent it to a "correspondent" bank, and such forwarding was repeated until the check reached a correspondent of the drawee bank who effected collection. The result was a fantastically complex and erratic procedure, since checks in process of either collection or remittance wandered up hill and down dale with many a stop and detour. Furthermore, the system had a built-in incentive to compound this abuse, for banks continued to have the benefit of a customer's deposit until final collection of both the customer's check and its own remittance had been effected.

These collection irritants were minor alongside the hazard involved in the concentration of reserve balances and temporarily idle funds in the large financial centers. The big city banks (after providing for their own reserves) put this cash to work, usually in the form of demand loans. As long as city and country demands for funds were synchronized, the system was valuable and efficient. When things got out of kilter, the withdrawal of money to the hinterlands could produce great discomfort in the financial and security markets. But over and above the recurrent strains in the flow of funds were the periodic panics. These were usually triggered by the failure of some large financial institution and entailed runs by banks on banks. The country institutions pulled their balances (reserves and all) out of the big city correspondents at the very time such funds were needed there the most, and the efforts at individual self-preservation provoked collective failure and collapse.

Banking and currency reform accordingly centered around the reserve question, and after almost a generation of backing and filling, the federal government began its fourth banking experiment on December 23, 1913, when President Wilson signed the Federal Reserve Act.[48] The act was a compromise between its predecessors, the first two of which set up massive central banks and the third of which involved no central bank at all. The Federal Reserve Act provided for eight to twelve regional institutions supervised by a government board, but with capital and deposits supplied by "member" banks. Their prime purpose was to hold the reserves of "member" banks in their respective territories. The concept of the federal monetary authority had advanced far enough by this time for compulsory membership in these regional banks (through stock purchase) to have been seriously considered for all banks, state and national. However, as finally passed, the act required only national banks to be members; state banks could join or not as the spirit moved them. Later, the act was amended to allow nonmember state banks to open special "clearing" accounts to permit them to send checks to and receive checks from a Reserve Bank. However, the heart of the reform was the provision, as the very name of the law suggests, that reserves would be maintained in the regional Federal Reserve Banks and the whole deposit system insulated, to a degree at least, from tremors in the financial centers.[49]

[48] 38 Stat. 251.

[49] The function of Reserve Banks was conceived by some as "mobilizing" these aggregated reserves and hence having them available for banks under pressure. Actually, a Reserve Bank's ability to supply reserves is not limited by the amount of assets which have been placed with it beforehand by others. Itself a bank of deposit, it can create reserves (up to its own fractional reserve limits as set by Congress) through its loan and investment operations. This brings in another aspect of the money power. Since the amount of reserves controls the upper limit of deposits, the power of the Federal Reserve Board to vary reserve percentages or the Reserve Banks to swell or restrict the balances means, in effect, that the federal government sets maximums on the quantity of money or money-equivalents.

We may note one other monetary function of the Reserve Banks. The bond-secured national bank notes were "inelastic." Relatively fixed in amount, they could not expand when commercial activity increased the demand for hand-to-hand money. A fluctuating supply of currency was provided by authorizing the Reserve Banks to issue notes against commercial paper representing the very business activity that provoked the additional demand. (The Reserve Banks could give this "money" in the form of reserve account entries.)

There were, however, similarities to past situations. Just as the second federal bank moved out to correct a deranged monetary situation of its day by a combination of persuasion and compulsion, so did the Reserve Banks take the field to organize the crazy-quilt pattern of check collection. They had been authorized to collect all checks their members might send them, subject to a prohibition against Federal Reserve payment of any exchange charges.[50] The account of a member bank with its Federal Reserve Bank thus served a double purpose. It was a "reserve account" since the balance measured compliance of the member with the amount it was required to maintain against deposits. It was also a "clearing account" since entries thereto were made by the Reserve Bank reflecting checks received from and sent to the member as well as other workaday banking transactions.

Thanks to superior facilities, the Reserve Banks managed to take over most of the collection business. However, a hard core of banks, mostly in the west and south, balked at giving up their "exchange charge" revenue and declined to cooperate. When persuasion failed, the Reserve Banks involved took sterner measures to discharge what they conceived to be their congressional mandate by taking checks

[50] There is some evidence that Senator Carter Glass inserted this prohibition in the Federal Reserve Act as a result of his experiences as a Lynchburg newspaper publisher: He developed an increasing distaste for having the proceeds of checks from out-of-town subscribers returned minus an exchange charge.

directly to the counters of these dissenting nonmembers and —as was their legal right at the time—demanding payment in cash and to the penny. The so-called nonpar (that is, exchange-charging) banks had no choice but to submit; to dishonor the checks would be to commit an act of insolvency. Accordingly, they sought the protection of the courts and the state legislatures.

Shortly before the roaring twenties got under way, a group of nonpar Georgia banks sought to enjoin the Federal Reserve Bank of Atlanta from this practice, which they said compelled them to keep large sums of idle cash and consequently reduced loaning operations. They went on to plead that the purpose of such presentations was to force them to take out membership or at least to open a Federal Reserve clearing account. The Reserve Bank did not admit the charge, but insisted that it was irrelevant to the legal right of a creditor to collect an acknowledged debt.[51] The trial and appellate courts agreed, and refused to grant the injunction. The case went on to the Supreme Court as a sort of latter-day *McCulloch* v. *Maryland,* and here our analogy seems to break down. The state banks won a temporary victory when the Supreme Court overturned the Federal Reserve's preliminary victory in a unanimous opinion, delivered by Justice Holmes, and declared that the question of motive was very much to the point:

> The defendants say that the holder of a check has a right to present it . . . for payment over the counter, and that however many checks he may hold he has the same right as to all of them and may present them all at once, whatever his motive or purpose. . . . But the word "right" is one of the most deceptive of pitfalls; it is so easy to slip from a qualified meaning in the premise to an unqualified one in the conclusion. . . .

[51] Actually, accumulation and sudden presentment of a competitor's notes were traditional and court-validated tactics of pre-Civil War banking.

. . . Banks as we know them could not exist if they
could not rely upon averages and lend a large part of the
money they receive from their depositors on the assumption that not more than a certain fraction of it will be demanded on any one day. If without a word of falsehood
but acting from . . . disinterested malevolence a man
. . . should . . . effect a run on a bank and ruin it, we
cannot doubt that an action would lie. A similar result
even if less complete . . . is to be expected from the
course that defendants are alleged to intend . . . it is not
enough to refer to the general right of a holder of checks
to present them but it is necessary to consider whether the
collection of checks in a body . . . is justified by the ul-
terior purpose in view.

. . . this is not a private business. The policy of the
Federal Reserve Banks is governed by the policy of the
United States with regard to them and these relatively
feeble contenders. We do not need aid from the debates
upon [the Federal Reserve Act] to assume that the United
States did not intend by that statute to sanction this sort
of warfare upon legitimate creations of the States. . . .[52]

While the opinion's bravura flourish of states' rights faintly
echoes the old Bank of Augusta case, all it really held was
that the complaining banks should have a chance to make
good on their assertion of "disinterested malevolence." The
case was accordingly sent back, tried by the lower court, and
dismissed on the ground that the Georgia banks failed to
prove what they had charged.

The Supreme Court upheld this finding.[53] On the very
day it did, however, it also upheld a North Carolina statute
which effectively ended mass over-the-counter collection of
checks on nonpar banks in that state and set a pattern for

[52] *American Bank & Trust Co.* v. *Federal Reserve Bank of Atlanta* (1921),
256 U.S. 350, 357–359.
[53] *American Bank & Trust Co.* v. *Federal Reserve Bank of Atlanta* (1923),
262 U.S. 643.

other jurisdictions.[54] The North Carolina law provided that a depositor, unless he otherwise specified, would be assumed to have authorized his bank to pay his checks with its own, that is, by tendering a draft on a correspondent bank. The statute contained a schedule of exchange charges and forbade en bloc over-the-counter collections. The state statute was challenged by the Federal Reserve on the ground (among others) that it attempted to nullify a law of Congress. But Justice Louis D. Brandeis, speaking for the Court, held there was no conflict. He found that the provision of the Federal Reserve Act authorizing the Reserve Banks to collect checks at par was no mandate to enforce universal par clearance, but merely a grant of permission to do so where they legally could. He went on to uphold the statute as an appropriate exercise of the state's police power in safeguarding the solvency of its banks.[55]

However, Justice Brandeis' opinion neither overturned the McCulloch case nor breathed new life in the inert Briscoe and Bank of Augusta decisions. Rather, it bore witness to what a change a century had made and how the roles of

[54] *Farmers & Merchants Bank* v. *Federal Reserve Bank of Richmond* (1923), 262 U.S. 649.

[55] The contention was also pressed that the statute made the paying bank's draft a legal tender in payment of debt in violation of the constitutional provision (Article I, Section 10, Clause 1). This the Court rejected on the ground that the statute merely created a presumption that the depositor (who could specify otherwise) authorized such mode of payment. These "legal tender" controversies—insofar as the states are concerned—form a minor element in our survey, but we may notice them briefly. Since a state retains control of its judicial machinery and procedure, it can make a creditor miserable and still stop short of invoking a legal tender provision. Thus, Kentucky made any creditor refusing Bank of Kentucky notes in payment of a judgment wait two years before obtaining an execution. Although the Supreme Court in the Briscoe case held that this point was not involved in the lawsuit, it suggested clearly enough that there was a difference between a tender that discharged a debt and a law that merely postponed payment. Over a century later the Court, in effect, validated a California statute which limited the amount of deficiency judgments on sales of foreclosed property to the difference between fair market value and the unpaid debt. Here, as in all of these situations, the difference between mere procedural provisions and outright legal tender is one of degree.

the parties in the McCulloch case had been exchanged: In the par clearance cases it was both the states and the state-chartered banks that were the "relatively feeble contenders," and the crux of the holding was that a federal agency had misconceived its duty, not—and emphatically not—that Congress could not give it such a mandate.

Perhaps the most meaningful text we could choose to sum up the completeness of federal authority over state banking would be a line from Justice Holmes' 1927 opinion in *Westfall* v. *United States* (concerning the power of Congress to make dishonest acts against state member banks into federal crimes): a "general proposition too plain to need more than statement." [56] We can complete the record by noting that the Supreme Court has refused even to listen to constitutional attacks on the Federal Reserve System and the Federal Deposit Insurance Corporation because of the impact of those organizations on state banks.[57]

This pattern of the par clearance cases, where a state's successful resistance of federal authority produced a judicial decision winning the battle and losing the war, was repeated a decade later when the Mississippi Supreme Court gave a minor setback to the monetary and banking program of the New Deal.

That program will be noted in some detail later; here it will suffice to recall that on March 6, 1933, two days after his inauguration, President Franklin Roosevelt acted under an almost forgotten World War I statute and ordered every bank

[56] 274 U.S. 256, 258.

[57] The Supreme Court has almost complete discretion as to the cases it will hear. It has warned time and again that its refusal to take a case does not necessarily mean that it approves the result reached in an inferior court. However, in view of the import of the major federal banking laws on state banking, it is impossible to avoid the conclusion that the Court's refusal to go into constitutionality of the effect on state banking of the Federal Reserve System (*Hiatt* v. *United States* [1924], 4 F. [2d], 374, certiorari denied 268 U.S. 704) and the Federal Deposit Insurance Corporation (*Doherty* v. *United States* [1938], 94 F. [2d], 495, certiorari denied 303 U.S. 658) was based on the obvious legitimacy of such relationships.

in the country, state and national, member and nonmember, to shut up shop and refrain from business activities.[58] There was considerable doubt whether the old statute provided a legal basis for the presidential proclamation. This doubt was, for all practical purposes, put to rest on March 9, when Congress passed enabling legislation for the holiday and purported to validate the proclamation from its inception.

However, before Congress acted, a supposedly closed Mississippi bank went out and foreclosed a mortgage. Its action was challenged as illegal and void, but the Mississippi Supreme Court held otherwise [59] on the grounds that the President had no power under the old World War I statute to close state banks and that Congress could not give retroactive validity to this action. However, the significant part of the Mississippi Court's opinion is not the Parthian shot of states' rights, but the declaration that once Congress had acted, the nationwide banking blackout was valid, constitutional, and final.

Notwithstanding the scope of congressional *power* over state banking, congressional *policy* has favored a coexistence of state and national systems. Thus, while membership in the Federal Reserve System or the Federal Deposit Insurance Corporation may involve some limitations on a state bank's corporate powers, such an institution is theoretically free to enter or quit either at its pleasure. Such freedom may be illusory in view of the almost universal popular demand for deposit insurance, but at least the voluntary nature of these arrangements shows how Congress has stayed its hand.

Actually, it has more than stayed its hand in an attempt to

[58] The statute in question was the so-called Trading with the Enemy Act (40 Stat. 415), which authorized the President during time of war or other national emergency (among other things) to regulate or prohibit transfers of credit or payments involving banking institutions. It provided also the legal base for the regulation of consumer credit in World War II.
[59] *Anthony* v. *Wiggins* (1938), 183 Miss. 885, 184 So. 626. Apparently no appeal was taken to the United States Supreme Court.

maintain parity between banks chartered under its authority
and those chartered by the states. For example, it has forbidden discrimination between state and national banks in the
deposit of federal funds. In a sharp turnabout from the death
sentence of 1865, it has provided that national banks, insofar
as branches and trust departments are concerned, shall have
only the powers possessed by their state-organized competi-
tors. This live-and-let-live attitude has resulted in American
banking which in a degree parallels the federal nature of
American government. This "dual banking system" has an
institutional character which obscures its slender legal base;
and under it, state banks have grown in number from the
two hundred and sixty-nine institutions of 1869 to the almost 10,000 that exist today and constitute over two-thirds
of all banks in the country. Yet it cannot be too strongly emphasized that all this manifests, not the cooperation of
equals, but the indulgence of a superior.

We need not trace the route of the money power to arrive
at the present federal dominance over state banks. It will be
recalled that Justice McLean, dissenting in the Briscoe case,
suggested an alternate route in his observation that all banking activities related "more or less" to interstate commerce.
This hint of the possible application of the commerce power
to state banking was seemingly scotched in 1850, when the
Supreme Court held that the business of lending money in
interstate commerce was not interstate commerce itself.[60]

However, the continuing integration of the national economy, so intimately bound up with run-of-the-mill banking
activities, meant inevitably that this decision would eventually fall. Its demise was provisionally forecast in 1942, when
a United States District Court in a wage-hour suit held that
modern commercial banking was interstate commerce.[61]
The decision was sealed when the Supreme Court refused

[60] *Nathan* v. *Louisiana* (1850), 49 U.S. (8 Howard), 73.
[61] *Lorenzetti* v. *American Trust Company* (1942), 45 F. Supp. 128.

to review the case.[62] Thus, state monetary power as manifested in commercial banking was doubly subordinated to the national government as federal authority over such institutions by virtue of the money power was reinforced by the federal authority to regulate all participants in interstate commerce.[63]

[62] 320 U.S. 770 (1943). Actually, the question of whether banking was interstate commerce was not pressed on the Supreme Court, though its review was sought on collateral matters. However, much of the reasoning in *U.S.* v. *Southeastern Underwriters* (1944), 322 U.S. 533, where the Court reversed a century-old precedent and held the insurance business to be interstate commerce, can be applied to banking.

[63] To complete the record, we might notice the quasi-monetary activity which is permitted the states. Thus a state can, without violating the "bills of credit" prohibition, make its taxes payable in coupons of its own bonds; *Poindexter* v. *Greenhow* (1885), 114 U.S. 270. And state treasurers can issue warrants against funds in their custody; *Houston R. Co.* v. *Texas* (1900), 177 U.S. 87. Moreover, a state can issue tokens to evidence payment of its sales tax without running afoul of the constitutional prohibition of state coinage; *Morrow* v. *Henneford* (1935), 182 Wash. 625, 47 P(2), 1016.

III

Public control
and individual freedom

No person shall . . . be deprived of life, liberty or property, without due process of law; nor shall private property be taken for public use, without just compensation.—Fifth Amendment to the Constitution of the United States.

Up to this point monetary authority has been considered in terms of its possessor, an analysis that is manifestly incomplete. Far more pertinent is the question of its exercise, since power necessarily involves the implicit or actual use of physical force against person or property. Within limits there is nothing pernicious about this. On the contrary, it is precisely the governmental monopoly of such force that underpins civilization. Without such force a political organization turns into a debating society, as the Articles of Confederation abundantly proved. Hence, the continuing and besetting problem of power is not its existence, but its magnitude, and the very division of governmental power between local and national instruments is but a means to a larger end of setting some tolerable limit upon force itself. Indeed the division, per se, is unimportant, for such power can be used as oppressively by a local government as by a national one.

Hence, we come to the core of the great constitutional design to provide both central and local governments with enough power to do their jobs but not enough to become intolerable tyrannies. To this end, the Constitution both gives power and takes it away. It takes it away specifically with respect to religion, assembly, speech, the press, jury trial, uncompensated expropriation, retroactive legislation, and the other areas of freedom specified in the Bill of Rights. It takes power away generally in a residuary provision forbidding government to take life, liberty, or property without "due process of law." The roots of "due process" run back at least as far as the Magna Charta, and in its evolved constitutional meaning it stands for the proposition that there are some things government simply cannot do. The ban applies both to the national government (through the Fifth Amendment) and the states (through the Fourteenth). "Due process" is not and cannot be a phrase of precision, for its scope and application must vary widely from time to time. But, however diverse its manifestations, the abstract central idea remains: Government cannot act arbitrarily. Government must use its power rationally, justly, and purposefully.

There is no exercise of governmental power, aside from actual deprivation of life or physical liberty, which is more keenly felt or more hotly resisted than its perennial assault on the purse. To adopt military parlance, we may say such assault takes two forms—the orthodox frontal thrust of taxation, and the infiltration-envelopment of monetary manipulation. It is on the latter theme that we resume our story by returning to the period of Civil War finance.

LEGAL TENDER: PRELIMINARY INTERDICTION

We may recall the action of Congress in foisting an issue of legal tender paper money on the unwilling Secretary Chase. The original hero or villain of this drama was an obscure New York Congressman named Elbridge G. Spaulding, who left his mark on history in the legend ". . . legal tender for all debts . . . ," which now appears on every piece of paper money issued under the authority of the United States. Spaulding had been increasingly disturbed by the growing discount that the government was encountering in the sale of its bonds. He feared Chase's original banking plan as a time-consuming venture that would immeasurably impede the war effort. He accordingly proposed a $150 million issue of legal tender currency notes, and his victory was won, for all practical purposes, when he overcame the constitutional reservations advanced by Thaddeus Stevens, chairman of the Ways and Means Committee and the forthcoming architect of the Reconstruction.

As we have seen, the Constitutional Convention left federal paper money as an open question, which Congress resolved by its 1812 issue of Treasury notes. Actually, more than twenty such issues were put out between 1812 and 1859, and Chase's original proposal for note-issuing banks showed his lack of objections to the paper money as such. It was legal tender that raised his original fears, and he could point to the precedent that in the darkest hour of the War of 1812 Congress decisively rejected a proposal to give this feature to Treasury notes. His objections were echoed by members of Congress who hotly challenged the constitutionality and economics of Spaulding's proposal.[1] Chase, however, finally

[1] The experience of Senator William Pitt Fessenden, chairman of the Senate Finance Committee, should deter us from a hasty judgment on the merits of the legal tender proposal. Fessenden had an open mind on the bill and sought

came up with a grudging endorsement as the Spaulding bill became an Administration "must" under the pressure of war finance. The proposal passed, was signed by Lincoln February 25, 1862; and thus after a lapse of almost a century, a legal tender paper money once more circulated legally in the United States.

In this respect, however, we must take care to assess laws in terms of their relationship to the world of reality. An assumption that legal tender as an actuality was absent from the United States between 1789 and 1862 goes wide of the mark. Legal tender exists in fact when a creditor must take an irredeemable token money worth less than the original value of the debt. We have seen how a state could use its court machinery to compel such settlements. This same result was reached by the application of community pressure working in extralegal channels. At many times and in many places between 1789 and 1862 the enforceable right to obtain gold in payment for a debt (either directly from the debtor or via bank notes given by the latter) simply did not exist. A creditor insisting on his legal rights could often face successive hurdles in getting a lawyer to plead his case, a local jury to return a verdict, and a sheriff to execute his judgment. Indeed, one history relates how a bank note-holder who insisted on gold redemption was hauled before the grand jury. This state of affairs is also manifested in the recurrent "suspension of specie payments" undertaken by the state banks, which theoretically should have closed

---

the counsel of two eminent financial experts, James Gallatin and Morris Ketchum. Gallatin wrote that the bill was not only useless but ruinous, and then hurried to Washington to drive his objections home by a personal appeal to the Senator to vote against it. When he arrived, Fessenden showed him Ketchum's reply to the effect that the bill was indispensable. Gallatin returned to New York and wired the Senator that he had changed his position and now supported the bill. The next post brought a letter from Ketchum changing *his* position to one of opposition. The legal tender proposal had a slim Senate majority, and Fessenden provided one of the five votes whereby it was enacted into law (12 Stat. 345).

them down. The continued operation of the banks meant that their notes circulated by community decree, so to speak, and not by the valueless legal covenant of the bank to pay off in gold.[2]

The Legal Tender Act locked Chase into the pattern of debt monetization as the pressure of financing sent him back to Congress again and again for authority to issue more legal tender notes. Legislative opposition dwindled with each request, and all recommendations were granted. However, the misgivings of both the Secretary and of the congressional dissidents seemed to be justified by subsequent events. Like their Massachusetts ancestors, the "greenbacks" (as the notes were called) started off at a discount, steadily declined through the year 1862, and then went through a series of rises and falls from face value in a manner roughly corresponding to the fortunes of the Union armies.[3]

[2] Something of a parallel in British history is recounted by Justice Joseph P. Bradley in his concurring opinion in the second Legal Tender case: "It is well known that . . . from 1789 to 1820, the most stringent paper money system that ever existed prevailed in England. . . . It is true that the Bank of England notes . . . were not technically made legal tenders, except for the purpose of relieving from arrest and imprisonment for debt; but worse than that, the bank was expressly forbidden to redeem its notes in specie, except for a certain small amount to answer the purpose of change. The people were obliged to receive them. The government had nothing else wherewith to pay its domestic creditors. The people themselves had no specie, for that was absorbed by the Bank of England, and husbanded for the uses of government in carrying on its foreign wars and paying its foreign subsidies. The country banks depended on the Bank of England for support, and of course they could not redeem their circulation in specie. The result was that the nation was perforce obliged to treat the bank-notes as a legal tender or suffer inevitable bankruptcy. In such a state of things it went very hard with any man who demanded specie in fulfillment of his contracts. A man by the name of Grigby tried it, and brought his case into court, and elicited from Lord Alvanley the energetic expression: 'Thank God, few such creditors as the present plaintiff have been found since the passing of the act.' It is to be presumed that he was the last that ever showed himself in an English Court." *Knox* v. *Lee* and *Parker* v. *Davis*, 79 U.S. (12 Wall.), 457, 568–569.

[3] Confederate notes followed the same "military" fluctuation. The Confederate Treasury was successful in defeating successive attempts to make its issues a legal tender. See Richard C. Todd, *Confederate Finance* (Atlanta: University of Georgia Press, 1954), pp. 118–119.

The Legal Tender Act was headed for the Supreme Court from the moment Lincoln signed it. An ironic historical twist made its reluctant endorser the head of that Court, for when Chief Justice Taney died in 1864, Lincoln told an associate that he was compelled to nominate a successor "who will sustain what has been done in regard to emancipations and the legal tenders." [4] His choice was Salmon P. Chase. Amendment of the Constitution took care of emancipation, but a rash of legal tender cases worked their way up the judicial ladder, and in due course gave the new Chief Justice the bitter choice of vindicating his record as a statesman or following his conscience as a judge. His resolution of the dilemma showed how a man convinced against his will retains his original opinion.

These "greenback" decisions began on January 16, 1869, when the Court decided *Bank of New York* v. *Board of Supervisors.*[5] This was a revenue suit growing out of a tax exemption that Congress had given the greenbacks. It involved a corollary of the McCulloch case to the effect that states could not lay a property tax on federal bonds. Ordinary money, however, had always been within the range of state taxation. New York claimed the exemption was unconstitutional on the ground that the greenbacks were nothing but money and, therefore, within the reach of its taxing arm. Speaking for a unanimous Court, the Chief Justice agreed that there was "much force" in this argument. Nevertheless, he concluded that the instruments were "strictly securities" and, hence, their tax immunity was perfectly constitutional.[6]

On February 8 the Court further whittled down the monetary status of the greenbacks in *Lane County* v. *Oregon,* and

[4] Quoted in E. S. Bates, *The Story of the Supreme Court* (Indianapolis: The Bobbs-Merrill Company, 1936).
[5] 74 U.S. (7 Wall.), 26.
[6] In 1894 Congress passed a statute (28 Stat. 278) which permitted nondiscriminatory state taxation of all circulating money issued under the authority of the United States.

through the Chief Justice held that the clause of the Legal Tender Act making the notes legal tender for all debts "has no reference to taxes imposed by state authority, but relates only to debts in the ordinary sense of the word. . . ." [7] The erosion continued a week later in *Bronson* v. *Rodes,* which involved a contract specifically requiring payment in gold and silver coin.[8] In his majority opinion the Chief Justice held that the agreement could not be satisfied by a tender of greenbacks of equal nominal amount. He pointed out that under federal law, coin continued to be a legal tender, that the government so used it, and that there was no express prohibition of such settlements in the Legal Tender Act. He concluded, therefore, that a specific commitment to pay gold was not a "debt" that could be satisfied by a tender of the notes. Chase then tipped his hand by observing it was not necessary for the Court to consider the constitutionality of the legal tender clause, which was the broadest of hints that the clause was unconstitutional and void.

At this point the unity of the Court began to dissolve. The Chief Justice's insinuation of unconstitutionality drove Justices Noah Swayne and David Davis to state that they concurred only in the result of the majority opinion rather than its implications, and suggested *their* belief that the legal tender provision was valid. Justice Samuel Miller broke into flat dissent, asserting that the congressional declaration of the notes as a tender for all debts meant precisely that and, moreover, was entirely within the legislative competence.

Hence, the division of the Court was forecast in preliminaries to the main event—or more precisely, to the first round of the main event, which began on December 10, 1869, with argument in *Hepburn* v. *Griswold* (hereafter

---

[7] *Lane County* v. *Oregon* (1869), 74 U.S. (7 Wall.), 71, 81.
[8] *Bronson* v. *Rodes* (1869), 74 U.S. (7 Wall), 229, whose rationale was reaffirmed by the Court in *Butler* v. *Horwitz* (1869), 74 U.S. (7 Wall.), 258, and *Trebilcock* v. *Wilson* (1872), 79 U.S. (12 Wall.), 687.

called Legal Tender I).[9] The case involved an $11,250 note signed in 1860 and due February 20, 1862, five days before the Legal Tender Act was signed. At both execution and maturity, gold and silver coin were the only lawful money in the country. When the note-holder finally sued in March of 1864, the debtor paid greenbacks (then circulating at about half their face value) into the local court and asked for a discharge. He did not get it and appealed.

The Supreme Court handed down its decision on February 7, 1870, and split 4 to 3 in holding that the Legal Tender Act could not apply to contracts made before its passage.[10] This was the only point for decision, although the majority opinion indicated the complete unconstitutionality of the legal tender clause. Both majority and minority agreed that the case was to be decided by the standards Marshall had laid down in the McCulloch case, namely, whether the purpose of the act was to give effect to specified power of Congress, whether the act was "plainly" adapted to achieve this purpose, and whether the act was consistent with the "letter and spirit" of the Constitution.

Moreover, the entire Court further agreed on the starting point of the inquiry: that the result sought by the act, means to the decisive suppression of the southern revolt, was a conceded authority of Congress. Unanimity dissolved when it came to applying this generality to particulars. Speaking for the majority, Chase vehemently denied that a legal tender money was "plainly adapted" to carrying on war:

> Certainly it cannot obtain new supplies or services at a cheaper rate, for no one will take the notes for more than they are worth. . . . The price will rise in the

[9] 75 U.S. (8 Wall.), 603.
[10] In effect the decision was 5 to 3. Justice Robert C. Grier, broken in body and mind, resigned on January 31, 1870, and did not technically participate in the decision of February 7. He had, however, indicated his concurrence with the majority before resigning.

ratio of the depreciation, and this is all that could happen
if the notes were not made a legal tender. But it may be
said that the depreciation will be less to him who takes
them from the government, if the government will pledge
to him its power to compel his creditors to receive them at
par in payments. This is . . . by no means certain. . . .

. . . whatever benefit is possible from that compulsion
. . . is far more than outweighed by the losses of property, the derangement of business, the fluctuations of currency and values, and the increase of prices to the people
and the government, and the long train of evils which flow
from an irredeemable paper money.[11]

The Chief Justice went on to assert that even assuming
that the greenbacks aided the war effort (a proposition he denied), the Legal Tender Act was consistent with neither the
spirit nor the letter of the Constitution. He held the cardinal
element of this spirit was the "establishment of justice,"
which found particular application in the sanctity of contracts and was correspondingly breached by any congressional attempt to impair them. His premises concerning the
letter of the Constitution were based on the provisions of the
Fifth Amendment forbidding private property to be taken
for public use without compensation, or for any purpose
without due process of law:

. . . if such property cannot be taken for the benefit of
all, without compensation, it is difficult to understand how
it can be so taken for the benefit of a part. . . .
. . . A very large proportion of the property of civilized
men exists in the form of contracts. These contracts almost invariably stipulate for the payment of money. And
we have already seen that contracts in the United States,
prior to the Act . . . were contracts to pay the sum specified in gold and silver coin . . . the holders of these contracts . . . are as fully entitled to the protection of this

11 *Hepburn* v. *Griswold* (1870) (*Legal Tender I*), 75 U.S. (8 Wall.), 603, 621.

constitutional provision as the holders of any other description of property. . . .

. . . [This Act compels] all citizens to accept, in satisfaction of all contracts for money, half or three quarters or any other proportion less than the whole value actually due. . . . It is difficult to conceive what Act would take private property without process of law if such an Act would not.[12]

Chase concluded with a moving apology for his own responsibility for the greenbacks:

It is not surprising that amid the tumult of the late civil war, and under the influence of apprehensions for the safety of the Republic almost universal, different views, never before entertained by American statesmen or jurists, were adopted by many. The time was not favorable to considerate reflection. . . . If power was assumed from patriotic motives, the assumption found ready justification in patriotic hearts. . . . Some who were strongly averse to making government notes a legal tender felt themselves constrained to acquiesce in the views of the advocates of the measure. Not a few who . . . acquiesced in that view, have, since the return of peace, and under the influence of the calmer time, reconsidered their conclusions. . . .[13]

Justice Miller, speaking for himself and Justices Davis and Swayne, took the opposite tack and stoutly upheld the Legal Tender Act as an "appropriate" means of carrying on the war:

It furnished instantly a means of paying the soldiers in the field, and filled the coffers of the commissary and quartermaster. It furnished a medium for the payment of private debts, as well as public, at a time when gold was being rapidly withdrawn from circulation, and the state bank currency was becoming worthless. It furnished the means to the capitalist of buying the bonds of the govern-

12 *Id.*, 75 U.S. (8 Wall.), 603, 623–625.
13 *Id.*, 75 U.S. (8 Wall.), 603, 625–626.

ment. It stimulated trade, revived the drooping energies of the country, and restored confidence to the public mind. . . .
It is now said, however, in the calm retrospect of these events, that Treasury Notes suitable for circulation as money, bearing on their face the pledge of the United States for their ultimate payment in coin, would, if not equally efficient, have answered the requirement of the occasion without being made a lawful tender for debts. . . .
. . . On the contrary, all experience shows that a currency not redeemable promptly in coin, but dependent on the credit of a promisor whose resources are rapidly diminishing, while his liabilities are increasing, soon sinks to the dead level of worthless paper. As no man would have been compelled to take it in payment of debts, as it bore no interest, as its period of redemption would have been remote and uncertain, this must have been the inevitable fate of any extensive issue of such notes.[14]

Justice Miller then went on to square the consistency of the Legal Tender Act with the letter and spirit of the Constitution. First, he vigorously contradicted the Chief Justice's conclusion about impairment of contracts:

. . . Congress is expressly authorized to establish a uniform system of bankruptcy, the essence of which is to discharge debtors from the obligation of their contracts. . . . How it can be in accordance with the spirit of the Constitution to destroy directly the creditor's contract for the sake of the individual debtor, but contrary to its spirit to affect remotely its value for the safety of the nation, it is difficult to perceive.[15]

14 *Id.,* 75 U.S (8 Wall.), 603, 633–634.
15 *Id.,* 75 U.S. (8 Wall.), 603, 637. Lincoln's five appointees to the Court, four mid-Westerners and a Californian, split 3 to 2 on the Legal Tender Act. The men universally conceded to be his best appointments, Samuel Miller, a physician turned attorney, and David Davis, a veteran judge from the Illinois courts, upheld the act, as did Noah Swayne, a corporation lawyer. Stephen Field, former Chief Justice of California, appointed after the act became law, joined Chase's opinion of unconstitutionality.

With respect to the letter of the law, he found the prohibition of the Fifth Amendment was too remote from the circumstances of the case to be applicable:

A declaration of war with a maritime power would thus be unconstitutional, because the value of every ship abroad is lessened. . . . The abolition of the tariff on iron or sugar would in like manner destroy the furnaces, and sink the capital employed in the manufacture of these articles. . . .
If the principle be sound, every successive issue of government bonds during the war was void, because by increasing the public debt it made those already in private hands less valuable. . . .[16]

Justice Miller insisted, moreover, that the law should be upheld on the precedent of the Veazie Bank case, protesting that if the congressional power over the currency permitted the destruction of state banking, it certainly covered legal tender. He concluded by denouncing the majority opinion's use of the "injustice" as a test of constitutionality, asserting that such injustice, "if it ever existed, will be repeated by now holding [the Act] wholly void" and in any event was too vague as a canon of interpretation:

It substitutes our [the Court's] ideas of policy for judicial construction, an undefined code of ethics for the Constitution, and a court of justice for the National Legislature.[17]

LEGAL TENDER: TURNABOUT AND TRIUMPH

The very day Legal Tender I was decided, two of President Grant's nominations for the Supreme Court were sent to the Senate. One was a replacement for Justice Grier. The other

16 *Id.*, 75 U.S. (8 Wall.), 603, 637–638.
17 *Id.*, 75 U.S. (8 Wall.), 603, 638.

was intended to bring the Court to a membership of nine, for Congress had reduced the number of Justices to preclude presidential appointments during its reconstruction controversy with the Johnson Administration, and had only recently restored the Court to its now-traditional complement. In March of 1870 the two new judges, Justices William Strong and Joseph P. Bradley, took their seats. Strong had come up from the Supreme Court of Pennsylvania, where he had written an opinion validating the Legal Tender Act.[18]

The reconstituted Court immediately called up two cases, *Knox* v. *Lee* and *Parker* v. *Davis* (hereafter called Legal Tender II), involving the issue seemingly settled once and for all only a short time before.[19] The two Grant appointees, in a momentous turnabout judgment of May 1, 1871, joined up with the three dissenters in Legal Tender I to reverse that decision outright and hold that the Legal Tender Act applied to pre-existing contracts after all. They went on to validate it as to contracts made after passage. The reports of this action are extraordinarily long, consisting of a majority opinion (Justice William Strong), a concurring opinion (Justice Bradley), and three separate dissents (Chief Justice Chase, Justice Nathan Clifford, and Justice Stephen Field).

A great part of this torrent of words merely elaborates the arguments previously exchanged, namely, that the Legal Tender Act was (or was not) an effective means of carrying on the war, and the act did not (or did) expropriate property "without due process of law." A new note appears in the acidulous personal tone that flavored the opinions on both

[18] Sixteen state courts passed on the Legal Tender Act. Fifteen upheld it; one declared it unconstitutional. Both Strong and Bradley had been railroad lawyers and exceedingly able ones. It is not indulging in the crude and vulgar inference that this background determined their judicial attitudes to point out that the heavy bonded indebtedness of the railroad system placed it in the debtor camp in the Legal Tender controversy and hence prevented that episode, like the Jackson-Bank struggle before it, from being labeled as a fight between the rich and the poor.
[19] 79 U.S. (12 Wall.), 457.

sides. The Chief Justice bitterly protested the reversal "unprecedented in the history of the court," while Justice Strong mentioned with evident relish the "historical fact that . . . the head of the Treasury represented to Congress the necessity of making the new issues legal tenders. . . ."[20]

However, some new elements of substance were added. Although Justice Strong, in simply rewriting the opinion he had previously delivered on the Pennsylvania Supreme Court,[21] put the main thrust of the majority opinion upon the plea of wartime necessity, he advanced two collateral lines of support. The first was the fact that the ability to pass legal tender laws was a power possessed by every other government in the civilized world, and would not be lightly denied the government of the United States. The second, closely related, was that the Constitution did not deny this power, but, on the contrary, granted it. Where and how? It was one of those powers that "grew out of the aggregate of the powers conferred upon the government, or out of the sovereignty instituted."[22] Although Strong cited Justice Story's *Commentaries on the Constitution* for this proposition, we immediately note that this was the very idea advanced by Hamilton (though for a different purpose) in his paper defending the constitutionality of the federal bank.

Justice Bradley delivered a powerful concurring opinion. Citing the Case of the Mixed Moneys, he endorsed the doctrine that the power of legal tender was implicit in sovereignty itself. However, he preferred to shift the emphasis of the majority opinion and place the thrust of his conclusion on the borrowing power by holding it a prerogative of every

[20] *Legal Tender II,* 79 U.S. (12 Wall.), 457, 572. The difficulty of the decision is manifested by the collapse in judicial manners. The decorum of the high court usually induces divided opinions to keep a more-in-sorrow-than-anger tone, and dissents conventionally begin: "When I have the misfortune to differ with my brothers. . . ."
[21] *The Legal Tender Cases* (1866), 52 Penn. State Reports 10, l. c. 56.
[22] *Legal Tender II* (1871), 79 U.S. (12 Wall.), 457, 535.

government to anticipate its resources via legal tender, not only in wartime but in other emergencies, unless restrained by a specific constitutional prohibition.

A practical reason for the latter logic lay in the fact that it tied the Legal Tender Act to a then-familiar American condition of recurrent suspensions of specie payments by commercial banks. In such periods banks did not necessarily close, nor did bank notes become valueless. The whole community recognized these situations for what they were—periods of temporary adjustment in which gold, though unavailable, continued to be the theoretical money of account and the ultimate standard of settlement.[23] The principal reason for Justice Bradley's separate opinion, however, was his inability to persuade a majority of the Court to say that Congress could, if it wished, make greenbacks payable for all debts, even those specifically calling for gold coin:

I do not understand the majority of the court to decide that an act so drawn so as to embrace, in terms, contracts payable in specie, would not be constitutional. Such a decision would completely nullify the power claimed for the government. For it would be very easy, by the use of one or two additional words, to make all contracts payable in specie.[24]

Vindication of Justice Bradley's prophetic remonstrance took almost three-quarters of a century. Otherwise, summary

[23] Both Strong and Bradley emphasized the temporary nature of the Legal Tender Act. Strong noted: "The Legal Tender Acts do not attempt to make paper a standard of value . . . nor do we assert that Congress may make anything which has no value—money. What we do assert is that Congress has power to enact that the government's promises to pay money shall be *for the time being* equivalent in value to the representative of value determined by the coinage acts. . . ." (Italics supplied.) *Legal Tender II,* 79 U.S. (12 Wall.), 457, 553. Bradley concurred: "[The Act] is not an attempt to coin money out of a valueless material, like the coinage of leather or ivory or kowrie shells. . . . The government simply demands that its credit shall be accepted and received by public and private creditors *during the pending exigency.*" (Italics added.) *Id.,* 79 U.S. (12 Wall.), 457, 560.
[24] *Id.,* 79 U.S. (12 Wall.), 457, 567.

reversal of the first legal tender decision was inevitable. Whether the two nominations which achieved that result were ingenuous or deliberate is one of the unsolved mysteries of American history. It might be noted, however, that the market place cast its vote against the action of the Court when the greenback price of gold remained relatively constant instead of falling in response to the deflationary implications of the decision. Technically, Legal Tender I decided only that pre-existing debts could not be satisfied by greenback payment. Actually, its major premise (as the Chief Justice and his followers clearly stated in their Legal Tender II opinions) required that *all* outstanding contracts calling for the payment of dollars, as such, be met by the delivery of gold or its equivalent greenback value.[25] In short, by virtue of the 25 per cent depreciation then prevailing, every debtor under an obligation to pay "dollars" would have been required to pay in greenbacks in a 4 for 3 ratio.

This requirement was instinctively rejected by the impersonal forces of the market, and its reaction was perhaps best manifested by the relatively few fluctuations in the dollar price of gold. Of a less impersonal nature, but still significant of the general refusal to accept Legal Tender I as a finality, was the policy of many corporations with respect to interest and principal payments on bonded indebtedness. Thus, one sampling of the financial policy of large railroads during the period shows that corporations tended to pay in currency and make provision for a subsequent gold "differential" payment upon the condition that Legal Tender I be specifically affirmed within a given period of time.[26]

[25] Chase was apparently troubled by this point and suggested that greenbacks would be a legal tender on those contracts "stipulating for payment in such notes" or calling for such payment "according to their terms." 79 U.S. (12 Wall.), 457, 583. The debts that met this requirement were few.

[26] See Charles Fairman, "Mr. Justice Bradley's Appointment to the Supreme Court and the Legal Tender Cases," *Harvard Law Review*, LIV (1941), 1128, 1149–1153.

There was, however, a countervailing consideration, which particularly appealed to the judicial conscience, and this was the oppressive force with which the act fell on people who had entrusted their fortunes to their government's money and so fell under a subtle capital levy, transferring their wealth to people who held an ownership of things.[27] As between them and debtors, who was to be penalized? Even Solomon himself could not have worked perfect *individual* adjustment here. Rather, justice had to be done at wholesale, and the crux of the settlement is contained in one sentence prefacing Justice Strong's opinion: "The debts which have been contracted since February 25, 1862 (the date of the Legal Tender Act), constitute, doubtless, by far the greatest portion of the existing indebtedness of the country." [28]

Although initiated as a wartime emergency measure, the greenbacks came to stay. Plans for their gradual retirement were upset by agitation against decreasing the currency supply—which finally carried the day in an 1878 statute forbidding further redemption and requiring reissue upon receipt by the Treasury. The statute was challenged in a creditor's suit, *Juilliard* v. *Greenman* (hereafter called Legal Tender III), which was decided in 1884.[29]

The plaintiff conceded that Congress could impress currency with the power of legal tender during wartime. He insisted, however, that the power was only as long as it was broad and lapsed when the war was over. The Attorney General and counsel for the debtor asserted as much in Legal Tender I when they referred to "this power-necessary for

[27] Justice Strong attempted to meet this point (but did so only halfway) in a quotation from Franklin: "The only consolation under the evil [depreciation of wartime currency] is that the public debt is proportionately diminished by the depreciation; and this by a kind of imperceptible tax, everyone having paid a part of it in the fall of value that took place between the receiving and paying such sums as passed through his hands." *Legal Tender II* (1871), 79 U.S. (12 Wall.), 457, 557.
[28] *Id.*, 79 U.S. (12 Wall.), 457, 529.
[29] 110 U.S. 421.

emergencies, pernicious as a constant resource." [30] The Supreme Court disagreed. Speaking for all the Justices save one (Justice Field stuck to the guns he had so stoutly manned since the Hepburn case), Justice Horace Gray asserted that Congress held such authority in both war and peace. The war-power base of the greenback, which was the heart of the controversy in Legal Tender I and began to diminish in Legal Tender II, was now relegated to further obscurity. In its place, Justice Gray took the Bradley thesis (that the legal tender power was a necessary consequence of the right to borrow on the national credit) and tied it to the whole range of specific congressional powers: war, foreign relations, coinage, and interstate and foreign commerce. But even more important was his declaration that the "when" of the use of the money power was no business of the Supreme Court:

> . . . the question, whether at any particular time, in war or peace, the exigency is such, by reason of unusual and pressing demands on the resources of the government, or of the inadequacy of the supply of gold and silver coin to furnish the currency needed for the uses of government and of the people, that it is . . . wise and expedient to resort to this means, is a political question, to be determined by congress. . . .[31]

When the Court says any action of the other coordinate branches of government involves a "political question," it is really admitting that the issues involved are beyond judicial remedy. To put the matter another way (and to revert to the provisional vocabulary adopted earlier), the Supreme Court's characterization of a controversy as "political" is its declaration that the power involved is a plenary one. Thus, the declaration of war by Congress involves a "political question"

---

[30] See Vol. 19, Lawyer's Edition, Supreme Court Reports, p. 516.
[31] *Legal Tender III* (1884), 110 U.S. 421.

par excellence. Examples can be multiplied endlessly: a state's apportionment of its congressional districts; the recognition of a foreign government by the President; the declaration by the Secretary of State that a constitutional amendment has been ratified appropriately; and so on. However varied their manifestations, "political questions" all carry the message of judicial nonintervention.

Thus, judicial appraisal of legal tender began by considering it as a provisional wartime expedient and closed by investing it with a legitimacy that was both permanent and beyond judicial control. Yet other Civil War actions of the federal government were initiated under the same plea of military necessity, and drew sharp judicial condemnation. Thus, the Court manifested its view of the civil repressions of the Lincoln Administration, when it freed a civilian who was imprisoned by a military tribunal and proclaimed:

> The Constitution of the United States is a law for rulers and people, equally in war and in peace, and covers with the shield of its protection all classes of men, at all times, and under all circumstances. No doctrine, involving more pernicious consequences, was ever invented by the wit of man than that any of its provisions can be suspended during any of the great exigencies of the government. Such a doctrine leads directly to anarchy or to despotism. . . .[32]

The foregoing language can be harmonized with the legal tender opinions, but reconciliation of texts is beside the point. Rather, the significant difference lies in the Court's power to safeguard individual civil liberties on one hand and its ability to make retroactive adjustments in complex economic legislation on the other. The difference comes down to this: A prisoner can be freed, but a million business transactions cannot be undone.

[32] *Ex parte Milligan* (1866), 71 U.S. (4 Wall.), 2, 120–121.

AN EXCEPTION TO LAISSEZ FAIRE

The Court did not use the canon of the "political question" to decide the next conflict between individual rights and monetary authority. Instead, it turned—at long last—to the "coin and regulate" clause of the Constitution when the case of *Ling Su Fan* v. *United States* was presented for decision.[33] Ling Su Fan was an ironic proceeding indeed. By way of background it can be briefly noted that the frontier philosophy of hard money underwent a complete turnabout as agrarian unrest manifested itself in successive demands for greenback expansion and unlimited coinage of silver at a ratio of 16 to 1. We know how the inflationist forces were decisively smashed in the election of 1896 and how the victorious McKinley Administration went from domestic to foreign triumph in the Spanish-American War and the acquisition of a ready-made overseas empire. Now the irony of the Ling Su Fan case lies in the fact that the imperialistic ventures of the "hard-money" McKinley Administration gave the defeated inflationists a legal precedent that over the long run was as valuable to their cause as any victory they could have won at the polls.

When the United States acquired the Philippines, Congress set up a commission to administer the civil government of the islands. The legislative powers of this commission were qualified by a restriction that enactments could not be made depriving anyone of life, liberty, or property "without due process of law," and, thus, specifically bound that body to the great guarantees of the Fifth Amendment. The commission adopted a silver coinage that was less than bullion

[33] *Ling Su Fan* v. *United States* (1910), 218 U.S. 302. It will be seen that the "coin and regulate" clause is a fairly late arrival in judicial assessment of the constitutional base of money authority. The first decision involving this clause seems to be the counterfeiting case, *United States* v. *Marigold* (1850), 50 U.S. (9 Howard), 560.

value, and forbade the export of silver coin from the islands. A Chinese resident tried to ship some coin out, was caught, convicted, and carried his appeal to the Supreme Court on the ground the export prohibition violated the assimilated constitutional guarantee by depriving him of property without due process. A unanimous court held to the contrary and affirmed his conviction:

> . . . it is said that if [a] particular measure . . . operates to deprive the owner of silver pesos of the difference between their bullion and coin value, he has had his property taken from him without compensation, and in its wider sense, without . . . due process of law. . . .
> Conceding the title of the owner of such coins, yet there is attached to such ownership those limitations which public policy may require by reason of their quality as a legal tender and as a medium of exchange. . . . They bear, therefore, the impress of sovereign power which fixes value and authorizes their use in exchange. . . .
> However unwise a law may be, aimed at the exportation of such coins . . . there can be no serious doubt that the power to coin money includes the power to prevent its outflow from the country of its origin. . . .[34]

The significance of this unspectacular case is immense, for it withdrew the monetary metals from a general doctrine that the Supreme Court had been developing over a quarter of a century. In 1872 the famous Slaughter-House cases laid down the doctrine that the grant of a slaughter-house monopoly by Louisiana did not deprive the unfavored butchers of their property without "due process."[35] The decision was based on the theory that the constitutional guarantee covered merely the right to hold property without molestation and nothing more. Exceptions crept into this reasoning as

[34] *Ling Su Fan* v. *United States* (1910), 218 U.S. 302, 310.
[35] 83 U.S. (16 Wall.), 36.

case after case was decided, and in 1897 the Court came full circle in *Allgeyer* v. *Louisiana* and held that "due process of law" protected not mere physical possession, but rather the right of access to a market.[36]

The 1910 term of the Supreme Court was a period of continued ratification of the general doctrine that the free market should not be impeded by either private combination or public interference. It was this historic term of the Court that produced the decisions of *Dr. Miles Medical Company* v. *John D. Park*, 220 U.S. 373 (striking down manufacturer's retail price agreements as offenses both at common law and under the antitrust act), *Standard Oil* v. *United States*, 221 U.S. 1 (divorcing a giant corporation from control of some thirty-seven subsidiaries), and *United States* v. *American Tobacco*, 221 U.S. 106 (similarly dissolving another gigantic enterprise).

Ling Su Fan provided an exception to these decisions. Its holding that the government could forbid an owner to export coin and realize its value on a world market was in fact a declaration that however precious metals might resemble property of the conventional type, differences outweighed similarities. The concession that Ling had "title" to the coins was more shadow than substance, for the decision held that such "title" was "impressed with the sovereign power" and carried "limitations which public policy may require." This holding burst whatever bounds restrained Legal Tender II and III, for those cases had insisted again and again that irredeemable paper was but a temporary expedient and that individually owned gold and silver coin was the permanent and enduring base of American money.

The same term of the Court produced another exception in favor of monetary authority over *laissez faire* in the case

[36] 165 U.S. 578. See also John R. Commons, *The Legal Foundations of Capitalism* (New York: The Macmillan Company, 1939), pp. 11–46, for the implications of the Allgeyer case.

of *Noble State Bank* v. *Haskell,* 219 U.S. 104, where the Court upheld an Oklahoma statute establishing a depositor's guaranty fund from assessments levied on banks. Here, Mr. Justice Holmes noted that "checks replace currency in daily business" and that this circumstance had profound implications on the whole philosophy of free-banking. Addressing himself to the question as to "whether the right to engage in banking is or can be made a franchise," he responded:

> . . . It is not answered by citing authorities for the existence of the right at common law. . . . We cannot say that the public interests to which we have adverted, and others, are not sufficient to warrant the state in taking the whole business of banking under its control. On the contrary, we are of opinion that it may go on from regulation to prohibition except upon such conditions as it may prescribe.[37]

THE SUPREMACY OF PUBLIC CONTROL

The legacy of Legal Tender II and III, the Ling Su Fan and Noble State Bank cases, was deferred for some time, but the implications of these decisions ultimately converged to give monetary authority a scope that had no limit but the sky. Unprecedentedly powerful forces were involved in the convergence: the stock market collapse of 1929 that turned an economic retreat into a rout; the collapse of European financial institutions that extinguished a flickering recovery and produced a persistent downward spiral of bankruptcy and liquidation.

Again we must summarize to the point of distortion, but we can get some insight into the nature of the disaster by fixing our sights upon one of its facets, the effect of the Great Depression on the free gold coin standard. We may recall

[37] 219 U.S. 104, 113.

that every monetary development—the bank note, the deposit account, the Federal Reserve System—was built upon this standard which presupposed the free movement of gold under private ownership throughout the country and indeed throughout the world.

Yet the very mechanism which for a century seemed to provide as good a monetary instrument as men were likely to get, now operated with a cruel perversity, and the house-of-cards banking and credit structure trembled as the cornerstone came under increasing stress. Each economic reversal sent more gold into hiding, pulled down the money supply, and depressed price levels. Each drop in the price level foretold another wave of disaster, for it meant that some group in the economy simply would not have enough income to meet obligations contracted at the older and higher levels.

We have already touched on one element of the remedial program, the bank "holiday" designed to stop the outflow of gold and to prevent the hopelessly lost institutions from dragging temporarily solvent ones down with them. A second element of the program was a radical revision of the gold coinage apparatus. The tactics of the over-all program were simple enough: first, to stop the escape of gold from the monetary base; second, to restore that which had previously escaped; third, to insure that such an outflow would not occur again; fourth, to restore the general price level to a point where yesterday's commitments could be met in terms of today's income; and fifth, to make sure that such readjustments were effective across the board. The action of the government proceeded accordingly. All privately owned gold and gold certificates were taken by the government; provision was made for a downward adjustment in the gold content of the dollar; and the prospective devaluation was made applicable to all existing obligations, as well as future ones.

The last step involved coming to grips with a unique

American institution, the gold clause. Largely as a result of the free-silver agitation of the late nineteenth century, apprehension of devaluation and attempts to avert its effects became a convention of American finance. This, plus the Bronson decision, caused a specification for repayment in gold coin of a given weight and fineness to be included as a matter of routine in all long-term debt obligations, including those of the government itself. Hence, the real thrust of the monetary revision was contained in a joint resolution of June 5, 1933, denouncing all gold clauses as "against public policy," forbidding their discharge in existing contracts, and making all coins and currencies of the United States legal tender.[38]

It was within this legal framework that January 17, 1934, became the deadline for the surrender of all gold into the treasury, and two weeks later the President, acting under delegated powers, devalued the dollar 40 per cent by reducing its defined gold content from 25 8/10 grains to 15 5/21 grains. Three creditors resisted. One was a railroad security holder, one the owner of a gold certificate, and the third the owner of a liberty bond. All of them, in effect, conceded the government's right to take their gold or, more precisely, to block their claims to gold; but they disputed

[38] Up to this time, dimes, quarters, and half-dollars were legal tender for debts up to $10; nickels and pennies were legal tender up to 25 cents. Federal Reserve and national bank notes had no legal tender power. For an interesting account of the possibilities the pre-1933 legal tender laws afforded, see Arthur Train's short story "The Doodle Bug" (*Mr. Tutt's Case Book*, New York: Charles Scribner's Sons, 1948, p. 305). Actually, however, the sharp practice of a last-minute insistence on a legal tender to slip out of a valid contract was given a hard blow by Justice Holmes in *Simmons* v. *Swan* (1927), 275 U.S. 113, where he indicated that under present-day custom anyone who insists on strict legal tender currency "instead of what usually passes as money" must give advance notice of such intention.

The Treasury has indicated that it is up to the courts to decide whether the 1933 legislation (38 Stat. 51; 48 Stat. 112) enlarged legal tender power of minor and subsidiary coins or withdrew such power from gold coins. See Treasury Department release, *Facts about United States Money*, September, 1959, p. 4.

its attempt to make them accept in return devalued currency of nominal equal value. Their claims were rejected by the Court on February 18, 1935. Chief Justice Charles Evans Hughes wrote all three opinions.

The Court commenced with the railroad bond involved in the case of *Norman* v. *Baltimore & O. R. Co.*,[39] noted that as a negotiable instrument it called for payment in gold as money and not as a commodity, and noted further that its gold clause was intended precisely to protect the holder against the very devaluation of the currency that had been effected. Conceding that this clause was a valid contract when made, the Chief Justice declared it within the protection of the Fifth Amendment, unless—and the "unless" was a big one—the congressional power which it attempted to anticipate and avoid could not be turned aside.

It will be recalled that the Legal Tender Act did upset rights acquired under contract, but whereas its impact might have been devastating in practical effect, this result, in contemplation of law, was nonetheless indirect. But in the present case the Court could not say, as it did in Legal Tender II, that the prohibitions of the Fifth Amendment were "too remote" to be applicable. Here the government stepped between the contracting parties and rewrote their agreement. The gold clauses could, therefore, be struck down only if they attempted to frustrate a dominant (or, in our terminology, "plenary") congressional power, as, for example, an agreement to pay a given freight rate despite whatever the Interstate Commerce Commission might prescribe, or an agreement to establish a monopoly made prior to the adoption of an antitrust act.

After a long review, ranging from the McCulloch to the Ling Su Fan cases, the Chief Justice concluded that the money power had precisely such a plenary character, and he concluded: "Parties cannot remove their transactions from

[39] 294 U.S. 240.

the reach of dominant constitutional power by making contracts about them." [40] The opinion then found that the gold clauses would require debtors to pay $1.69 in currency while receiving their income in that currency at par, and concluded:

> We are not concerned with consequences, in the sense that consequences, however serious, may excuse an invasion of constitutional right. We are concerned with the constitutional power of the Congress over the monetary system of the country and its attempted frustration. Exercising that power, the Congress has undertaken to establish a uniform currency, and parity between kinds of currency. . . . In the light of abundant experience, the Congress was entitled to choose such a uniform monetary system, and to reject a dual system. . . . The contention that these gold clauses are valid contracts and cannot be struck down proceeds upon the assumption that private parties . . . may make and enforce contracts which may limit that authority. Dismissing that untenable assumption, the facts must be faced. We think that it is clearly shown that these clauses interfere with the exertion of the power granted to the Congress, and certainly it is not established that the Congress arbitrarily or capriciously decided that such an interference existed. [41]

The Chief Justice next turned to the cases of the gold certificate holder, *Nortz* v. *United States*, [42] and the liberty bond owner, *Perry* v. *United States*. [43] Whereas the Norman case was in theory a dispute between private parties, the latter suits involved the United States as a defendant. This one salient fact was decisive, for it involved an elementary rule of law that no sovereign body—kingdom, republic, or state—can be dragged into its own courts without its permis-

[40] *Norman* v. *Baltimore & O. R. Co.* (1935), 294 U.S. 240, 308.
[41] *Id.*, 294 U.S. 240, 316.
[42] 294 U.S. 317.
[43] 294 U.S. 330.

sion. The rule has a corollary: If such permission has been granted, then suit can be carried on only under the precise conditions that the sovereignty has laid down. Congress had permitted suits against the United States on its contracts and had set up a special tribunal, the Court of Claims, to adjudicate them. It was here that Nortz and Perry filed their original petitions. The Court of Claims heard their cases, but did not settle them. Instead, it sent the controversies to the Supreme Court.

Nortz had argued that the enforced exchange of his gold certificate, representing bullion, for irredeemable paper deprived him of his property. Up to this part of the argument he had a point. He then went on to measure this loss by the difference that existed on January 17, 1934 (the date of surrender), between the world price of gold—assertedly $33.43 an ounce—and the $20.67 an ounce (predevaluation) price of gold coin to which the certificate entitled him.

Now the law does not and never did purport to offer reparation for every invasion of a legal right. Generally speaking, when a wrong produces demonstrable injury and this can be reduced to a monetary assessment on a showing of "before" and "after" values, the aggressor will be ordered to make a compensatory—but not a windfall—payment to his victim. Under certain circumstances such a money payment may be ordered without reference to the "before" and "after" test. Thus, so-called "nominal" damages may be ordered paid when the purpose is merely to vindicate the fact that a right has been invaded; sometimes "punitive" damages—those deliberately disproportionate to the injury—may be inflicted to make an example of the wrongdoer. However, nominal and punitive damages are the exception and not the rule.

The question of damages resolved the case. The certificate, the Supreme Court found, promised dollars, not gold, and dollars Nortz received. His attempt to use the world market

for an index of loss was unavailing. The Court decided on
the authority of the Ling Su Fan case that "plaintiff had no
right to resort to such markets. By reason of the quality of
gold coin 'as a legal tender and as a medium of exchange'
limitations attached to its ownership, and the Congress could
prohibit its exportation and regulate its use." [44] It accordingly followed that since the asserted measure of actual
damages could not be used, a decision against the government on any other basis would involve awarding "nominal"
damages. However—and here was the key to the whole
decision—Congress had not given the Court of Claims such
extraordinary jurisdiction. The Nortz suit was accordingly
dismissed.

This issue of damages also lifted the Court over its thorn-
iest hurdle—repudiation by the government of the gold
clauses in its own bonds, which was challenged by the Perry
case. The Court specifically denied that Congress could
adjust its own debts the way it had done with private contracts, since the Fourteenth Amendment provided that "the
validity of the public debt of the United States, authorized
by law . . . shall not be questioned."

Nevertheless, the Court held that the binding quality of
the government's promise presented a legal question distinct
from how much the bondholder could recover. The Nortz
case had already barred the world market price of gold as a
measure of asserted loss. This meant that the domestic price
level was the only available measure, or, as the Court put it,
"a consideration of the purchasing power of the dollars which
the plaintiff could have received." But unfortunately for the
plaintiff and despite the Administration's high hopes for its
counter-deflation program, the price levels had barely moved
from predevaluation lows. The Court accordingly dismissed
the suit on the ground that the "plaintiff has not shown, or

[44] *Nortz* v. *United States* (1935), 294, U.S. 317, 330.

attempted to show, that in relation to buying power he has sustained any loss whatever." [45]

This elaborate logic managed to uphold the government's repudiation of its own gold clauses, but went the long road home with its extended analysis of rights that had no remedies and prohibitions that did not prohibit. Justice (later Chief Justice) Harlan F. Stone reached the same goal by a much shorter step when he contributed his concurring note, tipping the balance on a divided Court:

> . . . it is unnecessary, and I think undesirable, for the Court to undertake to say that the obligation of the gold clause in government bonds is greater than in the bonds of private individuals or that in some situation not described and in some manner and in some measure undefined, it has imposed restrictions upon the future exercise of the power to regulate the currency. I am not persuaded that we should needlessly intimate any opinion which implies that the obligation may so operate, for example, as to interpose a serious obstacle to the adoption of measures for stabilization of the dollar. . . .
>
> There is no occasion now to resolve doubts . . . with respect to these questions. At present they are academic. Concededly, they may be transferred wholly to the realm of speculation by the exercise of the undoubted power of the government to withdraw the privilege of suit upon its gold clause obligations. . . . It will not benefit this plaintiff, to whom we deny any remedy, to be assured that he has an inviolable right to performance of the gold clause. . . .
>
> I therefore do not join in so much of the opinion as may be taken to suggest that the exercise of the sovereign power to borrow money on credit, which does not override the sovereign immunity from suit, may nevertheless preclude or impede the exercise of another sovereign power, to regulate the value of money. . . . [46]

[45] *Perry* v. *United States* (1935), 294 U.S. 330, 357.
[46] *Id.*, 294 U.S. 330, 359-361.

The Court was divided by more than which logic might
better support a decision for the government. Speaking for
himself and three associates, Justice James C.
McReynolds
cast a fond backward look at the dissents in Legal Tender II
and III ("The plan under review in the Legal Tender cases
was declared within the limits of the Constitution but not
without a strong dissent") and then leveled a blistering excoriation at the majority and concurring opinion:

. . . if given effect, the enactments here challenged
will bring about confiscation of property rights and repudiation of national obligations. Acquiescence in the decisions just announced is impossible. . . .

Just men regard repudiation and spoliation with abhorrence; but we are asked to affirm that the Constitution has
granted power to accomplish both. No definite delegation
of such a power exists; and we cannot believe that the far-
seeing framers . . . intended that the expected government should have authority to annihilate its own obligations and destroy the very rights which they were
endeavoring to protect. . . .

The [gold] clause is not new or obscure or discolored
by any sinister purpose. For more than 100 years our citizens have employed a like agreement. . . . From the
housetop men proclaimed its merits while bonds for bil-
lions were sold to support the [First] World War. . . .
It appears in obligations which have rendered possible our
great undertakings—public works, railroads, buildings. . . .

Counsel for the government and the railway companies
asserted with emphasis that incalculable financial disaster
would follow refusal to uphold . . . impairment and repudiation. . . . Their forecast is discredited by manifest
exaggeration. But, whatever may be the situation now con-
fronting us, it is the outcome of attempts to destroy lawful
undertakings by legislative action; and this we think the
Court should disapprove in no uncertain terms. . . .

Loss of reputation for honorable dealing will bring us

unending humiliation; the impending legal and moral chaos is appalling.[47]

Whatever the rationale which prompted the members of the Court to validate or denounce the government's repudiation of its own gold clauses, the important thing was that the government had won its victory for the time being. However, the basis of the majority opinion suggested an opposite result would be reached as soon as some bondholder was able to prove damages in terms of domestic purchasing power. This contingency, as Justice Stone suggested, was "transferred wholly to the realm of speculation" when Congress, as of January 1, 1936, withdrew the government's consent to suit on monetary claims, and so slammed and locked the door of the only tribunal in which demands might be brought.

An obscure corollary decision, the Holyoke Water Power Company case,[48] may be taken as an appropriate closing motif, since it provides a bridge to the past and a signpost to the future. This suit involved a lease containing a gold clause of a fairly complex nature—the renter was committed to pay annually, not gold coin, but *an amount of currency* which would purchase a quantity of gold equal to 1,500 dollars of United

---

[47] *Norman* v. *Baltimore & O. R. Co.* (1935), 294 U.S. 240, 361–381. One historian has noted that the five justices who upheld the gold legislation were Easterners and had spent most of their pre-judicial careers wrestling in some manner or other with the incredibly complex problems of urban and industrial societies. The four dissenters, on the other hand, were the products of frontier-type communities where vice and virtue were easily discerned and "root, hog, or die" summed up both an abstract philosophy and a way of life.

The reference of the dissent to the efforts of the "government and the railway companies" to sustain the gold clause prohibition again illuminates a point that has been touched on before, that debtors are not to be confused with the poor or dispossessed.

[48] *Holyoke Water Power Company* v. *American Writing Paper Company* (1937), 300 U.S. 324. The Court subsequently voided another "indirect" gold clause. In *Guaranty Trust* v. *Henwood* (1939), 307 U.S. 247, it voided an option of holders of dollar bonds to elect an alternate payment in guilders, pounds, marks, or francs as an attempt to tie a debt otherwise payable in dollars to a fixed value of particular money.

States gold coin of the standard fixed by law in 1894. The Court, speaking through Justice Benjamin N. Cardozo, struck down the elaborate calculus, held the mode of payment prohibited, and ordered the rent discharged by payment of $1,500 of paper currency:

In last analysis, the case for the petitioner amounts to little more than this, that the effect of the Resolution in its application to these leases is to make the value of dollars fluctuate with variations in the weight and fineness of the monetary standard, and thus defeat the expectation of the parties that the standard would be constant and the value relatively stable. Such, indeed, *is* the effect, and the covenant of the parties is to that extent abortive. But the disappointment of expectations and even the frustration of contracts may be a lawful exercise of power when expectation and contract are in conflict with the public welfare. . . . To [such] congenital infirmity this covenant succumbs.[49]

The four Justices who dissented so vigorously from the Gold Clause cases did not bother to submit an opinion in the corollary decision, but thus merely noted their disagreement with the result reached and so gave an illuminating index of how the outrageous passed into the commonplace. Acceptance of the decision did not mean a general abandonment of a search for contract forms that would yield "constant standards and stable values." On the contrary, the search accelerated as the various formulas and indexes of the government itself were pressed into service. Nevertheless, the Holyoke Water Power Company case is a constant reminder that wherever, whenever, or however monetary standards become involved in human affairs, the citizen may plan with

[49] *Holyoke Water Power Company* v. *American Writing Paper Company* (1937), 300 U.S. 324, 341.

imagination and subtlety, but it is the government that will dispose.[50]

It should be noted, moreover, that the 1935 Gold Clause decisions manifested the completion of a steady trend rather than a radical innovation in the Court's exposition of constitutional doctrine. In particular, it should be noted that they came *before* the Court's 1937 turnabout validation of the bulk of the New Deal program; and aside from the validation of the Tennessee Valley Authority, the gold legislation was the only item of major federal economic intervention upheld by the Court's 1934 and 1935 terms.

[50] We may note that holders of certain European obligations had better luck in enforcing gold clause payments in foreign courts. The reason was twofold. First, not many European issues contained a "gold clause," whereas it was put in American obligations as a matter of course. Hence, the aggregate economic effects of European judicial decisions were marginal. Second, while most European countries reduced the gold content of their currencies, none prohibited the exercise of "gold clause" rights, as did the American Congress.

IV

The money power: nature and implications

In forming a government which is to be administered by men over men the great difficulty is this: you must first enable the government to control the governed and in the next place oblige it to control itself.—James Madison—*The Federalist*, No. 51.

Justice Stone's trenchant concurrence in the *Gold Clause* cases (and here beyond all question is the core of the decision) brings us full circle to familiar ground. After allowance is made for the verbal differences of time and place, and "Congress" is substituted for "the King," it becomes clear that Stone merely laid down the doctrine of the Case of the Mixed Moneys. This is a hard doctrine and one not readily reconciled on its face with the basic ideas of American government. Indeed, the blunt ipse dixit with which the English court laid down the rule of the Case of the Mixed Moneys can be taken as a hallmark of the despotism which sent the American colonies into rebellion. Yet the rebellion eventually produced a government of its own, and in turn the problem of the nature and scope of the powers of that government.

On one hand were the bitter fruits of the arbitrary or capricious use of monetary authority by the governments of the American states. On the other was the undeniable fact that monetary authority was the power of a sovereign government; in the last analysis it must exist and can reside only there.

This situation made for a continuing dilemma which ran through a century and a half of American history, all too often being dodged rather than met. Witness, for example, the ambiguous silence of the Constitutional Convention; the roundabout logic of Hamilton and Marshall; Chase's painfully mingled convictions which took him down the path but prevented his taking the last logical step. Yet ultimate resolution of the problem did not spring on the scene unannounced. It had been prefigured time and again in the prophetic insights of Justices Johnson, Story, Strong, and Bradley.

Actually, the subsequent history of monetary authority is merely an exposition of consequences after Strong and Bradley reached the heart of the matter in Legal Tender II in their recognition that a government which concedes any power save its own within the area of its competence simply is not sovereign, and, for better or worse, the institution of money is by its very nature within that area. The government and only the government can declare what money shall be, emit it, enforce it, and protect it. In short, power is power. Within its limits it is, *ipso facto,* absolute, and the possibility of its abuse is simply irrelevant to the question of its existence.

Granting that monetary authority in all its manifestations is necessarily a function of national government, cannot its exercise be checked and tempered by that very government's judicial arm? We have seen the negative answer of history. At this point we may put our finger on the reason—partly legal, partly practical—why this is so. Judicial helplessness has resulted from the fact that every major exercise of the

money power of the national government has been validated
by the market place, which thinks in terms of dollars as dollars rather than units of some fluctuating and variable metallic content. In the market place, monetary relationships are
both the score and, indeed, a large part of the rules of the
game. To press our analogy, we may say that the game has
no quarters, no time-outs, and no closing whistle. The play-
ers' decisions must be made, and they must be made immediately. Participants continuously enter and leave; a myriad
of elections to buy and sell, to borrow and lend, and to take
future commitments on, occur in incessant, massive, and complex sequence.

If the government changes the monetary rules in midgame
(and it is always midgame), the results may be harsh and oppressive; but play must go on. It goes on without a priori
compensatory adjustments in payment and price by participants in the economic process. The adjustments come, of
course, but by the piecemeal and circumstantial market processes. Indeed, these market forces compel a recognition of
continuing identity of the monetary unit. In brief, the host
of participants who are tied to the past by both debts and
credits in the old money imperfectly recognize the new in
decisions and commitments to the future. There is no great
divide between the old and the new, but rather a mass of
imperfect understandings and adjustments of almost incredible magnitude and complexity.

To put this situation to rights is beyond even the great
powers of the United States Supreme Court. Hence, the
Court understandably stays its hand when faced with the
blunt consequences of rending the fabric of the economic
going concern by invalidating the new monetary rules after
they have been assimilated as practical facts of life. As Justice Strong suggested in Legal Tender II, the issue in that
case had already been decided by the preponderance of debt

contracted after the Legal Tender Act. Similarly, the Gold Clause cases, when all was said and done, merely offered the Court the opportunity to add about $70 billion to the debts of a people slowly emerging from the greatest depression in their history. In brief then, the mere passage of time put monetary changes beyond the power of the Court to undo.

Must this be? Cannot the Court stay the hand of the Legislature, either at the outset or so close to that point in time that the status quo is relatively unchanged when its judicial power is brought to bear? It cannot. And here we come to what the late Justice Jackson called "the most significant and least comprehended limitation" of judicial power. However useful advance or accelerated opinions may be, the Supreme Court simply cannot give them. Under the Constitution (Article III, Section 1), it can act only in "cases" and "controversies" and in practically all instances as an appellate court. That is to say, there must first be a bona fide lawsuit between adversary litigants, contested through a trial and (usually) through an intermediate appeal. And this, as any litigant can attest, takes time. When, and only when, all these preliminaries are over, the Supreme Court can assert its jurisdiction, but—as far as the money power is concerned—it is a jurisdiction which vanishes with the passage of time. The consequences were noted by Mr. Justice Jackson shortly before his death in 1954:

Two of the greatest powers possessed by the political branches, which seem to me the disaster potentials in our system, are utterly beyond judicial reach. These are the war power and the money, taxing, and spending power, which is the power of inflation. The improvident use of these powers can destroy the conditions for the existence of liberty, because either can set up great currents of strife within the population which might carry constitutional forms and limitations before them. . . .

No protection against these catastrophic courses can be expected from the judiciary. The people must guard against these dangers at the polls.[1]

[1] Robert H. Jackson, *The Supreme Court in the American System of Government* (Cambridge: Harvard University Press, 1955), pp. 59–61.

Synopsis of cases

American Bank & Trust Co. v. *Federal Reserve Bank of Atlanta* (1923), 262 U.S. 643. Suit by a commercial bank to restrain mass over-the-counter collection of checks by Federal Reserve. (Previous appeal in 1921 [256 U.S. 350] had held Federal Reserve activities were not to be tested by the law of private property and commercial bank was entitled to present evidence on Federal Reserve motivation.) Judgment for Reserve Bank on ground that no improper motives (e.g., compulsion to System membership) had been proved.

Bank of Augusta v. *Earle* (1839), 38 U.S. (13 Peters), 519. Suit on a note purchased by a bank outside its state of incorporation and payable outside such state. Judgment for the bank on the grounds that at common law, right of banking could be restrained or regulated only by the individual states and that the transaction in question contravened no state regulation.

Bank of New York v. *Board of Supervisors* (1869), 74 U.S. (7 Wall.), 26. Proceeding to collect state property taxes levied on United States notes (greenbacks). Judgment for the taxpayer on the ground that greenbacks were federal securities rather than money and hence exempt from state taxation.

Briscoe v. *Bank of Kentucky* (1837), 36 U.S. (11 Peters), 257. Suit to enforce payment of a note given for notes of a state-owned bank. Judgment for the bank on the grounds that its notes were neither issued by nor on the credit of the owner state and consequently were not state "bills of credit" prohibited by the Constitution. Dissent contains second explicit judicial reference to plenary federal monetary authority.

Bronson v. Rodes (1869), 74 U.S. (7 Wall.), 229. Suit to collect gold coin as specified for repayment in note. Judgment for the creditor on the grounds that Congress had not forbidden such contracts and hence legal tender greenbacks could not be forced in payment thereof.

Craig v. Missouri (1830), 29 U.S. (4 Peters), 410. Suit to collect a note given for a loan of state "loan certificates." Judgment for creditor on the ground that "loan certificates" were state "bills of credit" whose emission was prohibited by the Constitution. But see *Briscoe v. Bank of Kentucky*.

Davis v. Elmira Savings Bank (1896), 161 U.S. 275. Suit for preference, given by New York statute, for savings bank funds held by insolvent depositary. Judgment against preference on ground that statute could not apply to national bank.

Easton v. Iowa (1903), 188 U.S. 220. Prosecution of national bank officer under state statute denouncing receipt of deposits by insolvent bank. Judgment for defendant on ground that statute could not apply to national bank.

Farmers' & Mechanics' National Bank v. Dearing (1875), 91 U.S. (1 Otto), 29. Suit on a state usury statute. Judgment for bank on grounds that such laws had no application to national banking institutions.

Farmers & Merchants Bank v. Federal Reserve Bank of Richmond (1923), 262 U.S. 649. Suit by a state nonmember bank to enjoin mass Federal Reserve over-the-counter check collections against defense that state statute forbidding such collection was unconstitutional. Judgment for state bank on ground that Congress had not directed such Federal Reserve activity and state statute was valid exercise of police powers protecting banks against sudden withdrawals.

First National Bank v. Union Trust Company (1917), 244 U.S. 416. Suit to oust national bank from doing a trust business on ground that the latter lacked a "natural" connection with federal banking and monetary powers. Judgment for national bank on ground that business practice supplied the connection.

Gold Clause Cases, The. See *Norman* v. *Baltimore & O. R. Co., Nortz* v. *United States,* and *Perry* v. *United States.*

Hepburn v. *Griswold* (1870), Legal Tender I, 75 U.S. (8 Wall.), 603. Suit on a debt antedating the Civil War currency and involving rejection of previously tendered United States notes. Judgment for creditor on ground that debts existing before passage of the currency acts could not be compulsorily satisfied by a tender of United States notes (greenbacks) issued thereunder.

Holyoke Water Power Company v. *American Writing Paper Company* (1937), 300 U.S. 324. Suit for rent which was fixed at the number of dollars required currently to buy gold worth $1,500 of U.S. coinage of 1894. Judgment for tenant on grounds that both direct and indirect gold clauses had been outlawed by Congress and that rent could be paid by $1,500 in paper currency.

Juilliard v. *Greenman* (1884), Legal Tender III, 110 U.S. 421. Suit demanding coin payment on a note and rejecting previously tendered greenbacks therefor. Judgment for debtor on ground that Congress could constitutionally make paper money a legal tender for payment of debt in time of both peace and war.

Knox v. *Lee* and *Parker* v. *Davis* (1871), Legal Tender II, 79 U.S. (12 Wall.), 457. Suit demanding coin payment of debts contracted both before and after the Civil War currency acts. Judgment for debtors, reversing *Hepburn* v. *Griswold,* on the ground that Congress has constitutional power to issue paper currency and make it legal tender for debts contracted before and after such issuance.

Lane County v. *Oregon* (1869), 74 U.S. (7 Wall.), 71. Suit to collect state taxes in coin. Judgment for state on ground that "debts" to which greenbacks were made legal tender did not include state taxes.

Legal Tender I. See *Hepburn* v. *Griswold.*

Legal Tender II. See *Knox* v. *Lee* and *Parker* v. *Davis.*

Legal Tender III. See *Juilliard* v. *Greenman.*

Ling Su Fan v. *United States* (1910), 218 U.S. 302. Prosecution for unlawful export of coin from Philippine Islands. Judgment for the government on the ground that prohibitory statute did not deprive the coin-holder of property rights without due process of law.

McCulloch v. *Maryland* (1819), 17 U.S. (4 Wheaton), 316. Suit for state bank note taxes. Judgment for taxpayer on ground that the Bank of the United States was a legitimate exercise of the implied powers of Congress and that such institution and its notes were exempt from state taxes.

Mixed Moneys, The Case of the (1604), 80 Eng. Rept. 507 ("law" French); Sir John Davies Irish Reports 48 (English). Suit to recover standard English sterling promised in contract made prior to royal enactment setting coin of lower bullion value for Ireland. Judgment for debtor on ground that royal prerogatives over coinage supersede contrary provisions for payment in pre-existing private contracts.

Norman v. *Baltimore & O. R. Co.* (1935), 294 U.S. 240. Suit to recover value of stipulated gold coin payment of bond interest after Congress devalued gold content of dollar and made paper money standard for all debt payments. Judgment for debtor railroad on ground that congressional power over money superseded private contracts concerning methods of payment.

Nortz v. *United States* (1935), 294 U.S. 317. Suit to recover bullion value of gold coin previously deposited with Treasury and rejecting postdevaluation paper money settlement. Judgment for government on grounds that no damages in terms of domestic purchasing power had been shown to result from Treasury's failure to surrender gold coin.

Osborn v. *The Bank of the United States* (1824), 22 U.S. (9 Wheaton), 738. Suit to force return of property to the Second Bank of the United States, which had been seized for delinquent taxes. Judgment for bank on grounds that tax was invalid for reasons asserted in *McCulloch* v. *Maryland.* Dissent (on procedural point) contains first explicit judicial reference to monetary authority of the federal government.

Perry v. *United States* (1935), 294 U.S. 330. Suit on stipulated gold coin interest payment of Liberty Bond and involving rejection of devalued paper currency. Judgment for government on ground that no damage in terms of domestic purchasing power had been shown and Court of Claims had no jurisdiction for any other type of recovery.

State of Missouri v. *Duncan* (1924), 265 U.S. 17. Suit by national bank for appointment by state probate court as executor notwithstanding inability to comply with statutory conditions prescribed by state statute. Judgment for national bank on basis of federal statute granting national banks fiduciary powers of competing state institutions.

Veazie Bank v. *Fenno* (1869), 75 U.S. (8 Wall.), 533. Suit to collect a federal tax on state bank notes. Judgment for government on ground that notwithstanding discriminatory effect of tax, the power of Congress to establish national currency included power to prohibit competitive media.

Westfall v. *United States* (1927), 274 U.S. 256. Prosecution for criminal offense against state member bank of Federal Reserve System. Conviction affirmed on ground that national interest in Federal Reserve System permitted Congress to punish offenses against state member banks as federal crimes.

Bibliography

BOOKS

James Truslow Adams. *The Living Jefferson.* New York: Charles Scribner's Sons, 1941.

Norman Angell. *The Story of Money.* Garden City: Garden City Publishing Company, 1929.

Banking Studies. By members of the staff, Board of Governors of the Federal Reserve System. Baltimore: Waverly Press, 1940.

E. S. Bates. *The Story of the Supreme Court.* Indianapolis: The Bobbs-Merrill Company, 1936.

Charles Austin Beard. *Economic Interpretation of the Constitution of the United States.* New York: The Macmillan Company, 1947.

Ernest Ludlow Bogart. *Economic History of the American People.* Second edition. New York: Longmans, Green and Company, 1926.

S. P. Breckenridge. *Legal Tender.* Chicago: The University of Chicago Press, 1903.

Edward Arthur Coke. *Institutes.* Philadelphia: Robert H. Small, 1853. Vol. II, Section 335.

John R. Commons. *The Legal Foundations of Capitalism.* New York: The Macmillan Company, 1939.

Charles P. Curtis, Jr. *Lions Under the Throne.* Boston: Houghton Mifflin Company, 1947.

John Davies. *A Report of Cases.* Dublin: Cotter, 1762.

Davis R. Dewey. *Financial History of the United States.* New York: Longmans, Green and Company, 1903.

William Yandell Elliott. *The Need for Constitutional Reform.* New York: Whittlesey House, 1935.

Federalist Papers. Charles Austin Beard (editor). New York: Doubleday and Company, 1948.

Benjamin Franklin. *Autobiography.* New York: The Century Company, 1901.

Clarence P. Gould. *Money and Transportation in Maryland.* Baltimore: The Johns Hopkins Press, 1915.

Bray Hammond. *Banks and Politics in America.* Princeton: Princeton University Press, 1957.

Albert B. Hart. *Salmon Portland Chase.* Boston: Houghton Mifflin Company, 1899.

Charles Evans Hughes. *The Supreme Court of the United States.* Garden City: Garden City Publishing Company, 1936.

Robert H. Jackson. *The Struggle for Judicial Supremacy.* New York: Alfred A. Knopf, 1941.

Robert H. Jackson. *The Supreme Court in the American System of Government.* Cambridge: Harvard University Press, 1955.

John M. Keynes. *Monetary Reform.* New York: Harcourt, Brace and Company, 1924.

Ralph Korngold. *Thaddeus Stevens.* New York: Harcourt, Brace and Company, 1955.

Edgar Lee Masters. *Lincoln the Man.* New York: Dodd Mead and Company, 1931.

Lloyd Mints. *A History of Banking Theory.* Chicago: University of Chicago Press, 1945.

Broadus Mitchell. *Alexander Hamilton.* New York: The Macmillan Company, 1957.

Wesley Clair Mitchell. *A History of the Greenbacks.* Chicago: University of Chicago Press, 1903.

Money and the Law (Proceedings of The Institute on Money and the Law, 1945). New York: New York University School of Law and the Economists National Committee on Monetary Policy, 1945.

Richard B. Morris (editor). *Alexander Hamilton and the Founding of the Nation.* New York: The Dial Press, 1957.

Allan Nevins. *The American States During and After the Revolution, 1775–1789.* New York: The Macmillan Company, 1924.

Arthur Nussbaum. *A History of the Dollar.* New York: Columbia University Press, 1957.

Arthur Nussbaum. *Money in the Law.* Chicago: The Foundation Press, 1939.

Ross M. Robertson. *History of the American Economy.* New York: Harcourt, Brace and Company, 1955.

Fred Rodell. *Nine Men.* New York: Random House, 1955.

Arthur Schlesinger, Jr. *The Age of Jackson.* Boston: Little, Brown and Company, 1945.

Adam Smith. *The Wealth of Nations.* Modern Library Edition. New York: Random House, 1937.

Joseph Story. *Commentaries on the Constitution.* Fifth Edition. Boston: Little, Brown and Company, 1891.

W. G. Sumner. *A History of Banking in the United States.* New York: The Journal of Commerce and Commercial Bulletin, 1896.

Carl B. Swisher. *Roger B. Taney.* New York: The Macmillan Company, 1935.

Richard C. Todd. *Confederate Finance.* Atlanta: University of Georgia Press, 1954.

Paul M. Warburg. *The Federal Reserve System.* 2 vols. New York: The Macmillan Company, 1930.

Charles Warren. *The Making of the Constitution.* Boston: Little, Brown and Company, 1928.

Charles Warren. *The Supreme Court in United States History.* 3 vols. Boston: Little, Brown and Company, 1924.

Ray B. Westerfield. *Money, Credit, and Banking.* New York: Ronald Press Company, 1938.

Walter Wyatt. *Constitutionality of Legislation Providing for a Unified Commercial Banking System.* Nineteenth Annual Report, Federal Reserve Board, Washington, D.C., 1932.

PERIODICALS

Phanor J. Elder. "The Gold Clause Decisions in the Light of History." *Georgetown Law Review*, XXXIII, Nos. 3 and 4 (1935).

Charles Fairman. "Mr. Justice Bradley's Appointment to the Supreme Court and the Legal Tender Cases." *Harvard Law Review*, LIV (1941).

John E. Hannigan. "The Monetary and Legal Tender Acts of 1933-34 and the Law." *Boston University Law Review*, XIV (1934).

G. C. Hart. "The Gold Clause in United States Bonds." *Harvard Law Review*, XLVIII (1935).

Richard A. Lester. "Currency Issues to Overcome Depressions in Pennsylvania, 1723 and 1729." *Journal of Political Economy*, XLVI (1938).

Arthur Nussbaum. "Comparative and International Aspects of American Gold Clause Abrogation." *Yale Law Journal*, XLIV, No. 1 (1934).

Sidney A. Ratner. "Was the Supreme Court Packed by President Grant?" *Political Science Quarterly*, L, No. 3 (1935).

Walter Wyatt. "The Par Clearance Controversy." *Virginia Law Review*, XXX, No. 3 (1954).

GOVERNMENT DOCUMENTS

Documents Illustrative of the Formation of the Union of the American States. 69th Congress, 1st Session, House Document No. 398, 1927.

Facts about United States Money. Treasury Department, September, 1959.

The First and Second Banks of the United States. National Monetary Commission Monograph. 61st Congress, 2d Session, Senate Document No. 571, 1910.

The Origin of the National Banking System. National Monetary Commission Monograph. 61st Congress, 2d Session, Senate Document No. 582, 1910.

Date Due

MY 29'63
MY 24'64
MY 6 - '65
FE 1
AG 16'68
MR 5 - '75

Demco 293-5